To Our Readers:

INTRODUCING

OTABIND®

INTERNATIONAL

"The Book That Lies Flat"
— *User Friendly Binding* —

This title has been bound using state-of-the-art **OtaBind**® technology.

- The spine is 3-5 times stronger than conventional perfect binding
- The book lies open flat, regardless of the page being read
- The spine floats freely and remains crease-free even with repeated use

We are pleased to be able to bring this new technology to our customers.

Health Communications, Inc.

3201 S.W. 15th Street
Deerfield Beach, FL 33442-8190
(305) 360-0909

OTABIND®

INTERNATIONAL

The Netherlands

The Grown-Up Man

- Heroes
- Healing
- Honor
- Hurt
- Hope

John C. Friel, Ph.D.

Health Communications, Inc.
Deerfield Beach, Florida

John C. Friel, Ph.D.
Friel & Associates/Lifeworks
St. Paul, Minnesota

Library of Congress Cataloging-in-Publication Data

Friel, John C.
    The grown-up man: hurt, hope, healing, heroes, honor / John
C. Friel.
        p.   cm.
    Includes bibliographical references.
    ISBN 1-55874-179-8
    1. Men — United States — Psychology.   2. Fathers and sons —
United States.   3. Heroes — Psychological aspects.   I. Title.
HQ1090.3.F75 1991   91-17880
305.31′0973—dc20   CIP

Publisher: Health Communications, Inc.
                3201 S.W. 15th Street
                Deerfield Beach, Florida 33442-8190

Cover design by Robert Cannata

DEDICATION

To my father, Elden C. Friel; my brother, Richard E. Friel; my brother-in-law, William A. McIntyre; my son, David; my good friends Dan Ellwanger, Stan Huff, Dan Burrows, Darrell Griffin, Ron Tewksbury and my old and dear friend Larry Weiss.

SPECIAL ACKNOWLEDGMENT

I want to thank the people of the American Midwest not just for being here, but for being so stimulating, grounded and healthy, too. As a native Californian I once believed that nothing existed between my home in San Francisco and New York City. I have lived here for 18 years and I am 44 years old. Sure, I gripe about winter and mosquitoes. And I may move back to California someday. But I have found recovery here, a wife I respect and love and good friends. Most of all, I have found myself here.

Around the time of my own recovery beginnings, in the mid-70s, I attended a reception in Minneapolis for a California-based, nationally-known psychologist-guru who had a lot of the same small-minded parochialism that I had learned as a Californian. We got into a discussion about the Midwest versus California, and the guy was downright insulting, implying that those of us who live here were somehow behind the times, or worse. What I have noticed as my internal pendulum began to swing away from my own small-mindedness is that a lot of people in the Midwest are centered, solid and very creative; and that this guy was flashy, arrogant, lonely and numb beneath all his hype. I began to appreciate the Midwest much more as I got into recovery. After working with professionals as well as clients from these states for many years, I know why it is such a joy to live and work here. The winters may eventually drive me out, but I will always hold the people close to my heart.

Chungliang Al Huang, author of *Quantum Soup* and *Living Tao: Still Visions and Dancing Brushes*, and other marvelous works, put it well when asked why he lived in Illinois: "'For the corn.' I laugh. But I mean it. Although people on the coasts may be more searching, more questioning, more immediately interesting, I find that the corn-growing farmer-philosophers of Middle America have roots firmly planted and heads squarely on their shoulders."

ACKNOWLEDGMENTS

There are so many people who have touched my life over the years that it is difficult to know where to begin or who to include. Also there are people who have been important in my past who would not now be appropriate to include even though I would like to. If I offend someone by not mentioning them, it is not out of malice, but rather tact or forgetfulness.

I am grateful to all of the men who have been my clients: those I have worked with individually, those who have attended our Lifeworks Clinic and the men in my men's therapy groups. I cannot name any of you for reasons of confidentiality; but your stories, your hope, courage, anger, fear, hurt, shame, wisdom, joy, guilt, sadness, tears, laughter and mutual supportiveness inspire me, give me hope and continually recharge my faith in the goodness and "redeemability" of humanity. Thank you.

I am grateful to all of my friends, colleagues and fellow recovering folks who have been a part of my growth, my recovery and my professional development. A partial list would include my first male teacher at Ross Grammar School; my friends, Larry and Sandra Weiss, who have been in my life since our paths crossed at Marin Catholic High School in 1961; a couple of Jesuit priests at the University of San Francisco whose teaching challenged me to think and wonder and to have awe about creation; Lawrence Murphy and Robert Milligan, psychologists at USF who first turned me on to the field; my advisors and faculty at West Virginia University, John R. Nesselroade,

Paul Baltes, K. Warner Schaie, Hayne Reese and John Cone, who took on a frightened adult child from an alcoholic family as a graduate student and helped him develop a professional career.

I also want to acknowledge the many people who have been in my life at one time or another since then, especially Richard and Maureen Gevirtz, William E. Byxbee, John A. Austin, Stan Pollock, Larry Luttmers, Tom Etten, David Thomas, Ron Salzberger, Lou Guillou, Charlie Olsen, Ken B. Solberg, Marilyn Frost, Walter Ayotte, Tish Reddick, Mary Pietrini, Arlene Katchmark, Doug Sorensen, Lyndel Brennan, Lynda Winter, Diane Naas, Joanna Jacobs, Nelda Cain, Eileen Middleton, John Holtzermann, Fifi Burrows, Karen Albig-Smith, Suzanne James, Richard Farson, John Nolan, Ken Adams, Nickey Larson, Bruce Smoller, Virginia Leone, Joy Miller, Ruth Fishel, Rokelle Lerner, Charles Whitfield, Ann W. Smith, Tom and Jeanne Bartsch, Gisela Labouvie-Vief, Niki Fiedler, Dan Ellwanger, Stan and Margie Huff, Darrell Griffin, Ron Tewksbury, Kermit and Mary Dahlen, Linda Murdock, Evelyn Leite, Joe Westerheide, Erich Labouvie, Dan and Jennifer Burrows, Bob Ackerman, Joe and Sharon Cruse, Wayne Kritsberg, Judy McCaleb, Bill O'Donnell and Gretchen Kellogg. And thanks to Jim Maddock for being a fine man of integrity and honor, and a psychologist and teacher of rare quality.

I would especially like to thank the management and staff of St. Luke's Gordon Recovery Center in Sioux City, Iowa, The Recovery Source in Houston, Texas and Sierra Tucson in Tucson, Arizona for their high degree of professionalism and for their commitment to staff health, recovery and continued growth and development.

* * * *

Special thanks to Bob and Anne Subby for sharing New Year's Eve with Linda and me every year, for sharing their friendship and recoveries with us and for being a couple who honor, respect and love each other dearly.

* * * *

I want to thank all of the people at Health Communications, Inc. and the U.S. Journal Training, Inc., for their support, including Gary Seidler, Peter Vegso, Michael Miller, Luann Jarvie, Suzanne Smith, Andrew Meacham, Marie Stilkind and Lisa Moro.

* * * *

I am grateful to my family members for being in my life: my parents Elden and Alice Friel who have died but are not forgotten; my siblings and siblings-in-law, Rich Friel, Nancy McIntyre, Bill McIntyre, Steve Bateson and Margo Bateson; my parents-in-law Lloyd and Phyllis Olund; and assorted nieces, nephews and spouses of same, Brian McIntyre, Suzanne McIntyre, Carrie King, Steve King, John M. Friel, Mark Friel and Mary Friel.

* * * *

To my wife, Linda, and my children, Kristin, Rebecca and David, I thank you for being the most important people in my life and for showing me daily what it means to have courage, love and self-respect. I also thank Nik, my running buddy for the past 10 years. He sheds more now and has retired from running due to hip problems, but he goes with me in spirit and his eyes still light up from behind their haze when I enter the house.

ABOUT THE AUTHOR

John C. Friel, Ph.D., is a psychologist in private practice in St. Paul, Minnesota. He is national Director of the Friel Lifeworks Clinics, an intensive, short-term treatment program for Adult Child, Co-dependency, Addiction and related Family-Of-Origin Issues which is offered in St. Paul, Minnesota, Sioux City, Iowa, Orange County, California, Dayton, Ohio, Oklahoma City, Miami and Houston. In addition he is National Clinical/Educational Consultant for The Recovery Source In Webster (Houston) Texas, an inpatient, hospital-based treatment program for Addiction, Co-dependency and Adult Child Issues. He is also an Adjunct Associate Professor of Psychology at St. Mary's College Graduate Center in Minneapolis. Dr. Friel earned his B.A. in psychology from the University of San Francisco in 1969, and his Ph.D. in psychology from West Virginia University in 1976. He is a nationally recognized author, trainer, speaker and consultant in the areas of dysfunctional family systems, co-dependency, adult child issues, stress, addictions and men's issues. He has consulted with a wide range of hospitals, treatment centers, colleges and universities, corporations, small businesses, medical practices, law firms, nursing associations and government agencies throughout the U.S. and Canada. A native of the San Francisco Bay Area, Dr. Friel has lived in Minnesota since 1973.

He is co-author, with his wife, Linda, of two best-selling books, *Adult Children: The Secrets Of Dysfunctional Families* and *An Adult Child's Guide To What's "Normal."*

CONTENTS

PREFACE

As with the other books that we have co-authored, the case studies presented here are composites of people with whom Linda and I and our colleagues have worked throughout the years. If you see yourself in one or more of the examples I use, please know that it simply means that you are not alone in your pain or in your struggles.

Whenever I refer to my own life experiences, I have made every effort to share with you only those parts about which I feel relatively complete. I do this out of respect for me, my family and you. Some of my personal disclosures here may make an impact. I hope it is accepted in the spirit in which it is shared.

For many years I have tried to present lecture and written material in a way that is not biased toward either heterosexual or homosexual people. But I also need to say that I am not an expert on gay-lesbian psychology and will not try to present myself as such in this book. Much of the material here will be very appropriate for gay men, but some won't. I can say that my fondness, respect, compassion and empathy for men include the gay friends and clients who have enriched my life; my life would now be less were it not for them.

Lastly, I need to say that it was difficult at first to start a book knowing that Linda would not be my co-author. Much more than my wife, she is my partner, my pal, my best friend, my lover, my confidant, my colleague whose work I respect most deeply, my best critic and my most important ally. Although she is technically not the co-author of this book, she has contributed significantly to my development as a human being and a man; to my clinical insights about men, women and relationships and to the case studies and clinical materials presented in this book. She is one of the most highly skilled psychologist/therapists I know, and I am honored to say that we work side-by-side.

We will be writing jointly again on future projects.

John C. Friel, Ph.D.

ABOUT ME
AND THIS BOOK

On November 2, 1990, Gary Seidler of Health Communications, Inc., called to see if I would be interested in writing a book. I had been well-received at the U.S. Journal Training First Annual National Conference on Men's Issues held in Phoenix in April 1990, and Gary wanted me to put down on paper some of my insights about men. I was flattered, but I wondered if I was ready to do another book as quickly as he wanted it, and I told him that Linda and I had already begun a book.

I got scared, then excited, then scared again. Do I have enough to say? Am I qualified to write this book? Linda and several colleagues had been suggesting for years that I do a book about men. But there are already so many books out on men, I told myself. Then I realized that this was the same decision process that Linda and I went through with our first two books. Gary assured me that the new book we were working on could wait, and I decided to go ahead with the project. I told myself that I wouldn't be able to cover everything that I could conceivably cover in a book about men, and that I didn't have to be compulsive and perfectionistic about it in any event.

Am I an expert on men and men's issues? Well, it all depends on how you define "expert." First, I have not been a man all of my life. I was a boy during my childhood and also during part of my adulthood. I have been male all of my life, so maybe that counts for something.

Second, I have worked with men in psychotherapy and have conducted men's therapy groups for most of the past

10 years and I was in a men's group myself in the mid-1970s.

Third, I had a father and I had a brother, and I also have a 15-year-old son. That doesn't make me an expert on anything in particular, but it's important for you to know.

Fourth, I like the men friends in my life. I have several of them now, which is a sign of my own health and recovery, I believe. At one point in my life I felt closer to my women friends and had more women than men friends, unlike now. I was like a lot of dysfunctional men who say that women are more open to feelings, so of course a sensitive, caring man would be closer to women than to men, right? Wrong. What I discovered in my own recovery was that having more women friends than men friends was a symptom of my co-dependency and the emotional abuse and neglect that I experienced in my very typical suburban San Francisco Bay Area childhood. My men friends are very important to me now.

Fifth, I like the men who are my clients. I like the cognitive ones, the sensitive ones, the funny ones, the shut-down ones, the scared ones, the addicted ones, the co-dependent ones, the grandiose ones, the timid ones, the angry ones, the sad ones, the gay ones and the straight ones. I like all of them. They are typical men, struggling with typical "men's issues." They want relationships that are whole and fulfilling. They have trouble expressing certain feelings. Some are extremely successful in their careers, and some are moderately successful in their careers. Some are married, some are divorced, some are never-married, some are gay, some are straight, some are bisexual and some are confused about their sexual identities and preferences.

Currently I have three men's therapy groups which meet for two hours each week and constitute the core of my clincial work in private practice, along with the Lifeworks Clinics. Each week I also see some individual clients. Primarily men. Whenever I consider cutting back my clinical practice to do more speaking and writing, I never consider stopping my men's therapy groups. It's just too rewarding to work with those guys every week — to see them come into group angry, scared, baffled, manipulative and desperate — and then see them leave with a sense of integrity, brotherhood, connectedness and hope.

Sixth, I care about the future of manhood, both mine and others. Although that doesn't make me an expert in anything either, it gives me one heck of a lot of drive to sit down and write this book.

I have tried in this book to put in written form some of the things I have learned on my own journey to manhood and I have been taught by the hundreds of male friends and clients who have touched my life over the years. I know that there are also many other good books about men already on the market, and I encourage you to read some of them, too. I do not expect you to accept everything I say as "gospel," nor do I expect you to dismiss everything I say without first giving it some serious consideration. Even psychologists have pearls of wisdom to share now and then.

As with our other work, I simply ask that you read this book with an open mind; that you evaluate it not only intellectually, but also emotionally and intuitively. And let some of it percolate inside of you for a while. Sometimes the most important insights we get are the ones that we resist the most.

As I look over the chapters in this book, I can see much that I would like to have added, but I had to stop somewhere. I began writing from my heart and after a while tried to place a structure around the material so it would be readable.

As with all my writing, I do not use a ghostwriter and am responsible for all but some light editing. Therefore, I must take responsibility for what is clumsily written or organized as well as what is done well.

1

HOW WE HURT

You taught me to be nice, so that now I am so full of niceness, I have no sense of right and wrong, no outrage, no passion.

Garrison Keillor
Lake Wobegon Days

Men On The Way To The '90s

REVOLUTION OR REVOLVING DOOR?

n the mid-'70s, I was a young psychologist right out of graduate school, teaching at a small midwestern college and feeling intellectually caught up in the anti-war movement, the women's liberation movement, the men's liberation movement and the fringes of the sexual revolution, whatever *that* was. It was an exciting time to be alive, I thought. People were experimenting with communal living, the psychology of aging was coming into its own, and we all seemed to be concerned about poverty, education of the underprivileged, civil rights and all of the other social programs of The Great Society.

The momentum and energy of the '60s were still spilling over into the '70s. The hopes and dreams

3

for a new world order were being carried by a generation raised on television, Camelot, material comfort and excess, political repression and social injustice, de facto slavery, an atrocious war in Southeast Asia and the sting of the first presidential resignation in America's history. A revolution of social consciousness *and* disillusionment swept across the country at the same time that the American family was beginning to crack and crumble under the weight of dizzying technological and structural change.

This change in the American family was poignantly captured by director Barry Levinson in his touching historical tribute to his own family system. In *Avalon*, Levinson created a movie that is a poetic documentary spanning 80 years of hope, family strength, rapid cultural change, the breakup and fragmentation of the extended family, the magic of boyhood, and above all, the wondrous flexibility and adaptability of the human race.

From the 1960s to the 1990s a lot of things changed but some only temporarily. There seems to be a dialectic to change, in which we swing from one end of a continuum to another and then land somewhere near a balanced center. For men and women, some of the changes had cruel outcomes.

For example, one of the most tragic developments in history, the subjugation of women, is still evidenced by grossly unfair differences in pay between men and women. But I have also seen unforgivable damage done to women *by* women, and by women to themselves, in the name of women's liberation, when women felt shamed if they chose to "stay home and raise children."

I once saw a woman in the name of ideological correctness, reduce her husband to shreds because he wanted to go duck hunting as he and his father had years ago. At the time, it wasn't politically acceptable to hunt ducks and so her husband gave up hunting and with it let another small part of his spirit die out, all in the name of liberalism. The real issue wasn't even about hunting. It was about their past experiences — his lack of fathering and her lack of mothering.

In addition I once saw a "humanistic-democratic" father in the name of political righteousness, destroy his son's ego in front of his family because he had voted for the "wrong" Senate candidate.

"Don't you have any sense?" he raged at his son. "The guy you voted for doesn't care about the poor, the down-trodden, the oppressed or the abused. Now you've really disappointed me!"

I watched this man tear out his son's heart and stomp on it in the name of the oppressed and the abused, and it felt really, really crazy! I looked on, numb.

CRAZY-MAN BELIEFS

I think many of us in 1975 believed that we had this whole man-woman thing figured out. But figuring something out and living a sane life can be two different things. In getting this stuff all figured out, I and many of my peers had some pretty crazy beliefs, too. For example, I thought that men's liberation meant that . . .

1. I had to cry as easily as many women do before I would be whole.
2. I had to become self-less and self-denying in the face of centuries of oppression of women and I also had to deny my feelings in the process. (I fully support quotas to make up for years of job unfairness, but I also know now that if I lose out on a job because I am male, I have the right to be scared, angry, hurt and jealous. I now know that normal human feelings are okay, too.)
3. I had to apologize for being male. I felt I had done something wrong because a Y-carrying sperm fertilized the egg instead of an X-carrying one.
4. I had to become demasculinized and a victim. I got that all mixed up with vulnerability and power, both of which are healthy.
5. I always had to put women first.
6. Little boys should not be encouraged to play football, while little girls should.

7. Sex was, if not downright dirty, at least something that was exploitive of women.
8. I was not attractive to women.
9. I had to "pay" for men's domination of women throughout history.
10. There was something wrong with me if I liked fishing, scary movies, mud, Clint Eastwood, working on cars and a million other "male" things (even though I also liked going to the symphony, reading a good book, romantic dinners, cooking and a host of other "female" things).

I had actually taken the unhealed wounds of my childhood, wrapped them in a blanket of social ideology and then proceeded to do the exact opposite of what I had done before, thereby creating a self and life that were just as dysfunctional as before. There is a saying in recovery circles that fits well here: *180 degrees from sick is still sick!*

CONFESSIONS OF A RECOVERING PSYCHOLOGIST

You see, back in the mid- to late-'70s, I wasn't just caught up in the excitement of rapid social change. There was much more going on inside of me. There were frightening feelings, behaviors that made no sense and pain that I was increasingly unable to keep at bay. So while I preached the importance of men's and women's liberation, what was bubbling to the surface of my consciousness was that I was an Unrecovering Alcoholic and an Adult Child Of Two Chemically Dependent Parents. Of course, these were *minor* problems next to the Vietnam War and Women's Equality, or so I thought. I bumbled and stumbled through life, teaching my college classes quite poorly, addicted to thinking and relationships as much as alcohol, got a divorce, experienced the deepest pain of my life up to that point and failed to see the big picture that was not outside of me, but inside.

For me, strong support of the Women's/Men's Liberation Movement was really about the unhealthy fathering and mothering that I received as a child. It was my acting out of a big chunk of family-of-origin dysfunction from my childhood. But I didn't know that at the time. Looking back is always easier than looking forward.

For example, we can look back and see that the anti-war movement was not only about an unjust war. For some, it was about students who had grown up in an era of permissiveness and wealth and who had time on their hands and anger in their hearts at their neglectful parents. The sexual revolution and women's movement in the '60s and '70s was as much about technological change and the advent of birth control as it was about "higher consciousness."

LOST SELF/LOST NATION

During the '70s, I became immersed in the work of Erik Erikson, especially his theories of identity development, because at some level I knew that I had no real identity. When Gail Sheehy's bestseller, *Passages: Predictable Crises Of Adult Life*, based on the work of Erikson, Levinson and Gould hit the bookstores in 1974, I read it with relish and smugness, secure in the knowledge that I had achieved my identity and was on my way to high level intimacy.

Yet in truth, I was *foreclosed*, in Erikson's terms. My identity development was all in my head, not in my reality, and it showed. I was in massive denial about my alcoholism, about the emotional abuse and neglect in my childhood, about the destructive relationships that I kept getting into and about how I was passing it all on to my own children. I was living a theory, not a life. One day I thought I had it all together; the next day I wasn't sure I'd even make it another day. What I found out much later was that the emotional roller-coaster I was on was an exact replica of the emotional experience of my childhood. It's what we call in family systems theory, a *re-enactment*.

In our civilized cultural arrogance, a lot of us believe that our humanness is better than our primitive ancestors'. We feel we are light years more evolved than cavemen and cavewomen, rather than just 30,000 years more evolved (which is a drop in the bucket compared to our planet's history). In fact, we are much more like our primitive ancestors than we would like to believe. The older and wiser I become, the more I am convinced of this fact. And the more I stay in recovery, the more I feel bonded to all of humanity, rather than to just the folks in my house or in my neighborhood. That is the real beauty of healthy recovery programs.

Erik Erikson believed that America was built on a foundation that skipped *basic trust*, the first of his eight stages of development. He felt that we are missing the most elementary part of our foundation, leaving us with a very shaky house.

So I will mention one more revolution in America that I believe is not a fad or a manipulation by big health care corporations: the 12-Step self-help movement of support and recovery modeled on the original 12-Steps of Alcoholics Anonymous begun in 1935 by Bill W. and Dr. Bob. I believe that these movements are a direct and healthy response to this lack of basic trust, and that they are beginning to heal the deepest wound of all in America, the inability to be intimate.

Due to the pioneering work of Margaret Cork, Claudia Black, Sharon Wegscheider-Cruse, Bob Ackerman, Janet Woititz, Vern Johnson, Cathleen Brooks, Jael Greenleaf, Bob Subby and many others, alcoholism became a treatable disease while the families of alcoholics and other addicts discovered there was a reason they were hurting, too. From family systems therapists such as Murray Bowen, Salvador Minuchin and Virginia Satir, we learned how families operated from the inside out. In addition Alice Miller's books on child abuse and neglect have ensured that we will never again be able to pretend that abuse does not exist.

WHAT DID I LEARN?

In my recovery from my addiction and from the abuse that I experienced as a child growing up in a dysfunctional family, I learned a number of other important things about myself and the men's and women's movements to which I had become so attached.

1. I discovered that my alcoholism was probably genetic to a great extent, appearing on both sides of the family. I also discovered that it was a good deal about emotional pain, too. Alcohol abuse became not only one of my best allies, but also a survival tool that kept me alive during young adulthood. I often say in lectures now that I wouldn't be alive today had I not become alcoholic, but that I also wouldn't be alive today had I not gone into recovery.

2. I discovered that parts of my identity were indeed relatively whole, but that chunks of it were not. As my willingness to surrender to my disease(s) increased, the fragmented parts of my identity started coming together more and more.

3. I discovered that my intense emotional connection to the women's/men's lib movement was about two deep psychological dramas unfolding inside of me. One was my attempt to be unlike the destructive parts of my father, which caused my rejection of the good parts of him as well. The other was my continued attempt to rescue my mother, who I mistakenly viewed as helpless and weak, when in fact she was powerful and seductive.

4. I discovered I could no longer live in a world where ideas were more important than human dignity. Denial and enabling are just as bad, or worse, when they come from a well-educated person, myself included. I realized that although I had a Ph.D. in psychology and a respectable job, I was emotionally and spiritually stuck back in childhood.

5. I found that the more I acted out my pain and "looked crazy," the more I catapulted myself toward my own recovery.

6. Then, as I stuck with the pain of moving headlong into all of this stuff instead of running from it, I found that life was very much worth living. I learned that my dignity as a person did not depend on my credentials or my politics. That men have a lot to teach women and that women have a lot to teach men. That *both* men and women get hurt in our society, and that we can help each other deal with the pain if we respond to the human dignity inside each of us.

7. Most wonderful of all, I found that the seemingly mundane, trivial things in life, such as a smile from a friend, the smell of fresh coffee brewing in the kitchen, a jog in the park with my dog or a warm silly private morning with Linda are what keep me connected to the earth, to myself and to the humanity all around me. I found that sitting in a 12-Step meeting for an hour each week let me stay humble and grateful, and that by doing so, I embraced healthy power. I could surrender to things more powerful than myself, thereby releasing all of that Fighting-Struggling Energy (as I call it) for more productive pursuits, like writing this book.

SOME BELIEFS EMBRACED IN THIS BOOK

I believe that each generation of men and women tries to improve on the previous one. This keeps me going when things look especially bad. I know that without help, many of us make it worse for our children even though we set out to improve. Social revolutions always start out with the best of intentions, and hopefully end with some improvements in society.

If we look at the evolution of childhood in the way that Lloyd deMause did in *The History of Childhood*, we can see that over the last 2000 years we *have* become more humane and caring. It is indeed a comforting thought. Ideology and social movements are not all bad by any means. They are the means to improve a culture. But it is important to remember that we all are individuals, too. We have faces, names, feelings and our own needs that get caught up in these movements as well.

In reality, every generation or so has a political and social "revolution." There is a new men's movement afoot in America that seems to be growing out of the co-dependency and recovery movement. As with all movements, there will be those who learn from it and improve, those who don't and before it is over, we will all become confused by it. It has taken me a long time and a lot of pain to know that beneath the rhetoric and the power struggles of a "revolution," there are real, flesh-and-blood human beings with real hearts and minds, with real souls and real dreams. It is also crucial to remember that human beings are individuals. They should not be abused or shamed due to another's belief system. So to summarize some of my beliefs about all of these things we have just discussed, I should say that I believe that . . .

1. All human beings are trying to grow toward health and self-actualization. At a spiritual level it is the same process for men and women, but at an earthly, physical and cultural level, men and women have some strengths that are different and some healing issues that are different.

2. Men and women will always have dynamic tension between them and this tension is good. The saying "You can't live with them and you can't live without them" will be as appropriate 3,000 years from now as it was 3,000 years ago.

3. Men's/women's liberation is (a) a social, political and evolutionary phenomenon and (b) a struggle for individual growth and healing of childhood wounds. Confusing the two can be dangerous.

4. Human beings will always struggle to improve and at least in this life will never be perfect.

5. With the exception of transsexuals, men shouldn't try to be women, and women shouldn't try to be men, but men and women both need to become more whole.

6. Sex-role stereotyping is unhealthy, as is *any* stereotyping. Imposing one's enlightened ideologies on another is also unhealthy.

7. Role-models are absolutely necessary for men and women to grow up whole but gurus are absolutely dangerous.

8. The important things in life are quite often those that seem trivial and mundane.

9. Apologizing for being male or female has nothing to do with a healthy social movement. Correcting dehumanizing beliefs and actions by society has everything to do with a healthy social movement.

ON THE EDGE OF HOPE

We have experienced huge losses as Americans over the past 30 years. We watched in horror as one after another of our most beloved leaders was gunned down in senseless violence. We were ravaged by a war that ultimately didn't make sense. We had a president resign in shame. We saw families fragment and a nation become addicted to drugs, alcohol, sex, food, work and television. We have done so much damage to our environment because of our excesses and our greed, it will take a near miracle to save ourselves at this point. Instead of getting better, the plight of the poor and underprivileged has become significantly worse over the past ten years. We have insane policies about ownership of handguns. And now we even find ourselves losing significant ground in the one domain in which we always excelled: the competitive marketplace.

We know how to fix things. We know how to destroy things. We know how to conquer others and take their land away from them. We even know how to know. But we have been shamefully poor at relating to each other as whole beings who have bodies and souls, as well as minds. I believe that as a nation we have "hit bottom," as we say in addiction circles, that we are perched on the edge of destruction *or* on the edge of more health than we have ever experienced before in our history. *The decision is up to us.* And as with any addiction, the only way we can begin to heal is to admit in all our fear and our shame that we have a problem. In other words, America needs to surrender to its unmanageability.

That, I believe, is the key to men's issues as well. We need to surrender to our weakness, and in so doing, we will recover the true healthy power that is part of *manhood*.

2

Over-Mothered, Under-Fathered: The Betrayed Male Syndrome

CULTURAL ROOTS AND FAMILY ROOTS

here was a lot of man-bashing in the '60s and '70s. Many men came to apologize for being male and internalized the shame of generations of men who had abused women. The ideology of gender liberation got distorted for many of us so we went to the other extreme. We gave *all* of our power to women in an attempt to make up for having too much in the past. Women complained that macho men were useless. At the same time, a lot of men became disillusioned with their own fathers. Dads who worked too much, who felt too little and who provided but didn't seem to know how to love, left a generation of men lost, hurt and angry about being men while being angry with their fathers, too.

There was an even deeper dynamic going on here because the wives of these Dads who couldn't feel or communicate wanted and needed a man around who could feel. Without really knowing it, those Moms gave a powerful covert message to their sons. The message was:

"I am disappointed by males. I am disappointed by your father. I secretly hate men. Be my little spouse and make up for it. Become a sensitive little man to please Mommy, and you will make Mommy happy forever. But know that while you are pleasing me, I will despise you and fear you and hate you because you are male, while in the same breath I will seduce you into being the sensitive, gentle male I have always longed for. I love men and hate them. I fear them and desire them. I need you, but I need you under my thumb, where I secretly wish I could put all men."

Of course, in any ongoing friendship or lover relationship, the two parties involved are of equal health and equal dysfunction and are unconsciously in collusion with each other, so the Dad in this system also has a powerful covert message to give to his son:

"My son, I need you to run interference for me with Mom because her needs frighten and overwhelm me. I never learned to be comfortable with my vulnerability or the vulnerability of others, so I will leave it up to you to take care of this for me. You are so good at it. Besides I need to be out making a living. So stay by Mom, be her surrogate husband. Listen to her problems. Become gentle and sensitive. Fill in all of those gaps. You will turn out okay. Trust me. Oh, wait. One other thing. Because you will become a sensitive male, I will not like you or respect you. I will fear you as I fear your mother. I will see you as "wimpy," and I will secretly hold you in contempt. But son, it will work out. Trust me."

Can you see how confusing it was for men back in the '70s? Society was telling us to become less macho; the women in our lives were telling us to get more sensitive and feeling-oriented. Then beneath all of that we had this crazy dynamic from our family of origin in which we were pawns in a battle between Dad's and Mom's unmet needs.

To top it all off, what do you think happened next? The women in our lives got confused as well. They said they wanted sensitive, gentle men, but then they got angry and disappointed with us if we weren't strong enough. It's not that they wanted macho men again, but it was certainly not wimpy men they wanted, either. What do women want, we began to ask ourselves. This is nuts!

Well, not "nuts" perhaps, but certainly painful. In fact, over the past 20 years I have seen literally thousands of men in this country who have fallen victim to both the covert, emotional incest dynamic described above and the women's liberation dynamic described above. It has been an especially confusing time for us because of this dual dynamic. Men and women lost in rapid social and technological change. Boys and girls caught in their parents' unconscious conflicts and frustrations. Dads and Moms using their children to meet their own adult needs instead of facing each other as intimate adults. And lots and lots of pain.

THE BETRAYED MALE SYNDROME

Don't get me wrong, though. I don't think that the past 30 years have been all bad for men and women. We have managed to make a lot of important and necessary and very healthy changes since 1960. But many men and women were not quite so lucky. Many of us are still confused, hurt, angry and scared. Especially so are men who suffer from being *over-mothered* and *under-fathered*. It is this dynamic, I believe, that causes so many men so much pain. It is this dynamic which causes so many boys and men to renounce their maleness. And by renouncing his maleness, a man renounces his identity and his power. Once a person renounces his/her identity and power, all that can remain is abuse of self, abuse of others, serious dysfunction, painful relationships and little personal dignity.

Over-Mothered/Under-Fathered

In the following pages I present what I feel are some of the key characteristics of men who have suffered from this dynamic. As you read, please keep in mind that some of these traits can also be caused by other family dynamics; that if you are struggling with any of them, I strongly urge you to seek professional help. They can each be quite destructive to self or others, and they are each quite treatable with family-of-origin/family systems therapy. We can choose to work through the pain and confusion, in other words.

Some of the traits of a man who has been over-mothered and under-fathered are the following:

1. Lacks "essential maleness"
2. Questions own sexual preference/gender identity
3. Overly masculinized/homophobic
4. Sweet guy/nice guy
5. Passive-aggressive
6. Female dependent
7. Rager
8. Rescues women
9. Hates women
10. Used/victimized by women

1. Lacks "Essential Maleness"

Essential maleness, as I call it, is that little corner of our psyches reserved "just for men." (See Chapter 7.) It is very difficult to define, and it surely has cultural modifiers. It is an elusive concept, yet whenever I bring it up, everyone in the audience nods and smiles in recognition. Essential maleness is what distinguishes men from women psychologically, regardless of whether the person is gay or straight. It is some kind of edge, detachment, vision or quality of perception that makes men different from women. It is that little voice deep down inside of even the most domestic and acculturated male that says, "I'd like to join Will Steger on one of his wilderness adventures," or

"I'd like to be on the first expedition to Mars," or "I'd like to lead an army or command a Fortune 500 company," or "I'd like to write the definitive work on Abraham Lincoln," or "Even though I'm opposed to hunting on moral grounds, at an emotional level a part of me would like to bring home a trophy buck some day . . . just once."

Having essential maleness does not mean being a beer-guzzling, rude, insensitive, sexually-addicted jock. It does not mean being intellectually-addicted to ideas so that one's passion and creative life force is numb or absent. It is that part of us which lets us cry unashamed at a friend's funeral, but in a way that does not invite smothering or pity. It lets us be proud of our bodies, our sexuality and our identities as men. It lets us guide others gently yet firmly. It lets us expand outside of ourselves, to build and create in responsible ways. It is that part of us which can be separate and alone without having to medicate ourselves with drugs, sex, work, food or relationships. *It is that part of us that makes us men.*

2. Questions Own Sexual Preference/Gender Identity

Gender identity has to do with whether we believe that we are a man or a woman. Sexual preference has to do with being heterosexual, bisexual or homosexual. Many men who had inadequate fathering and over-mothering have difficulty with either gender identity or sexual preference. When a client states that he isn't sure about these issues, I tell him to wait and see what emerges after he does some significant work around family-of-origin issues of fathering, mothering, abuse and the like.

I don't know many professionals who consider homosexuality to be an emotional problem. It was removed from the category of a clinical diagnosis years ago. From all that I've read and surmised from my gay clients, homosexuality is something that is most likely biological, i.e., simply a biological variation of sexual expression which is within the realm of normal behavior. If it bothers you that I say this, there is nothing that I can do about it, except to encourage you to examine your own beliefs about sexual preference.

In any event, men who have had insufficient parenting have a very difficult time deciding on sexual preference, and sometimes even have a difficult time with gender identity. If you think about it, this makes sense because a man who didn't get enough fathering will not have learned how to be male as he was growing up. Thus part of his recovery will be to get the fathering he never got.

3. Overly Masculinized/Homophobic

This man is what we used to call the "macho man." He is on the "very dysfunctional" end of the list of male traits, so that we might describe him as rough, tough, a ladies' man (which usually means sexually addicted and female dependent), aggressive, unethical, ruthless, unfeeling, uncaring, perhaps charming in a boyish kind of way, reckless, emotionally blunted. This guy is probably described as "all boy" by his parents and "all man" by his friends, but what he is really experiencing is terror and profound loneliness. This man is likely to be physically and emotionally abusive, especially to women.

In addition, he will be terrified of homosexuality, a feeling which will only get worse as he tries to deal with his own emerging sexuality. In reality, sexual preference is actually on a continuum, with most of us somewhere in between heterosexual and homosexual. This will be frightening to the overly masculinized man, as will most feelings, especially the "vulnerable" ones. I assume that this is the guy to whom women refer when they say that the only feelings men are capable of feeling are anger and lust.

This type of distorted maleness can also arise out of over-fathering by an overly-masculinized man married to a woman who is caught in the victim role. In the case of over-mothering and under-fathering, it is a man's angry response to abandonment by his father and enmeshment with his mother.

4. Sweet Guy/Nice Guy

Without adequate fathering to teach him how to have healthy male power and with his mother demanding covertly that he be only gentle and sensitive, a boy may slide into the role of the sweet guy/nice guy. Many women at first glance believe that they have captured a truly liberated man when they begin to date him, because he seems to be operating at a feeling level all the time. Actually, most of the men in this mode are stuck in their heads and talk about feelings but rarely have clear expression of feeling. Eventually, the woman in his life discovers that this man is trapped in a mode of always trying to please, which makes intimacy impossible and which makes her very angry, because nobody wants to be with a "pleaser" for long.

Rather than having healthy power, this man will yield and yield and yield some more, until he's had enough. Then he will intermittently explode into a rage.

Because he has been abandoned to Mom by Dad and has been emotionally seduced by Mom, this man will continue to fall in love with seductive women who use him, take advantage of him and then discard him, which repeats the painful pattern of his childhood bonding over and over again. Without intensive treatment for the complicated childhood wounds he has suffered, this man will continue to have painful relationships both with women and men. To heal from this pain, it is essential that this man get the fathering that he didn't get as a boy, which can happen in a men's therapy group and with a male therapist who is healthy.

5. Passive-Aggressive

Similar to the sweet guy/nice guy, a passive-aggressive man isn't able to express anger directly or clearly and has great difficulty asking for what he needs. He therefore expresses his anger indirectly by pouting, punishing with silence and withdrawal of love or attention, pained sighs and rolling of eyes in disgust. Being around a passive-aggressive man or woman is very uncomfortable. We feel crazy, scared or angry most of the time because what the person communicates verbally is the opposite of what he or she communicates nonverbally.

6. Female Dependent

This is sometimes difficult to spot and sometimes not. Men who are female dependent feel inside they cannot exist without a woman in their lives. If the man has been hurt a lot in childhood, this dependency will be handled by allowing a female child to become his surrogate parent. A man's overdependency on a woman can be manifested by a sense of neediness or helplessness that she picks up, even though he would probably protest loudly that he "doesn't need or want a woman in his life." Men who are female dependent will often be very powerful and controlling with women, either because of brute strength, money, age or other forms of power. It can be manifested in helplessness around the house and needing a woman to do domestic tasks for him, and can show up in a man who needs a woman to feel his vulnerable feelings "for" him ("for" is in quotes because it is a contradiction to say that someone can feel feelings "for" you). A woman with a female dependent man in her life will ultimately feel used, ripped off and smothered. She won't get what she bargained for. Then she'll leave.

7. Rager

There are many reasons for men's rage. Some of it is justifiable anger at the intrusiveness or abusiveness of one's family or loved ones. Rage can be a response to repeated boundary violations, especially when you have asked the violator to stop more than once. It can be a response to verbal, emotional and intellectual abuse, which are more subtle boundary violations. Rage is often a response to a mother who smothers a boy year in and year out. It can also be a response learned by watching Dad, who was also a rager, or by watching Mom, who was also a rager. But for many men, rage is a cover for something much deeper. It can be a powerful, deceptive cover for hurt, shame and fear. Many ragers, both men and women, are really acting out their hurt, shame or fear. These feelings are vulnerable ones and we do not feel safe expressing them, so we cover them with a fraudulent power—our rage.

8. Rescues Women

This is one of the most common and most debilitating results of emotional incest with Mom. We see Mom unhappy. Perhaps we see Dad hurting her and neglecting her. Mom unconsciously lets us into her world and we become her Little Savior. Before we know it, we're out in the world unconsciously finding dysfunctional women who are as bad off as we are, who we can then rescue and try to fix. We feel so gallant and saintly, powerful and needed as we slip into the role but it really damages us. Moms and Dads aren't supposed to be rescued. Dads and Moms are supposed to take care of us!

9. Hates Women

I remember an episode of *The Little Rascals* when I was six or seven years old. The Rascals formed a club called the He-Man Woman-Haters Club, and it seemed perfectly okay at the time. After all, at those ages, little boys and little girls hang out in same-sex groups a lot. But when a man carries real hatred for women into adulthood, it isn't cute anymore. A man's hatred of women in adulthood can be seen in sexual addicts who use and objectify women, in corporate bosses who discriminate against women managers, in men who batter women and in men who are terrified of women and find female sexuality disgusting. We see it in men who think of women as slaves and second-class citizens. We see it in men who don't value women's opinions, feelings, beliefs or ideas. It shows up in men who believe that women "owe" men something, such as their bodies.

10. Used/Victimized By Women

Many men who get used by their Moms and aren't protected by their Dads end up being used and victimized by women. We rescue them, only to find them to be offenders themselves. Many a Mom's Little Man has been seduced and taken advantage of by a sexually addicted woman, by a woman unable to make commitments, by a rageful and controlling woman or by a woman who just wants a guy she can push around. It is difficult to know how to avoid this trap because it's just a re-enactment of our relationship with Mom. But it *can* be untangled.

A colleague of mine, Ken Adams, has written a book on emotional/covert incest in both men and women, *Silently Seduced: When Parents Make Their Children Partners*, outlining the many ways that we can get hurt by having to be parents to our parents. The pain that results from being over-mothered and under-fathered is a deep one. In fact, Robert Bly's book, *Iron John*, is devoted almost entirely to this pain at one level or another. I encourage you to read Adams' and Bly's books and begin to feel your way through the maze of childhood messages you received from Dad and Mom. If you get lost along the way, do ask for help. It can make all the difference in the world.

3

Silly Things That Dysfunctional Men Do

ecause we men often tend to be rational and logical, sometimes the best way to help us see how to make change in our lives is to appeal to reason and logic. That seems logical to me anyway. As I look back at many of the painful ways that I lived in the past, hindsight lets me see the folly of much of it. But it was also foresight that helped me to change much of it.

I remember one week that Linda took my men's groups for me a few years ago when I had back surgery. She visited me in the hospital the next day and one of the things she said made me want to sit up and take notice even though I was in too much pain to actually do so. She said that in some ways she found men more workable in therapy than women.

She admitted it might simply be a trait of the men in my group or of men who had got that far in their healing process. She had noticed that like women, men get pretty stuck with the feelings stuff, but that once they made a decision to get on with their recoveries, they seemed to go at it with gusto. I do believe there is some truth to it. If one of our faults is being too rational and decisive, there must be a positive side to it as well. Deciding to change is a huge part of healing for anyone.

Truly seeing the folly of our beliefs and actions can be a powerful incentive to change. Facing the inconsistencies between what we feel, what we say and do and what we think can be a powerful way to get through our denial barriers and start moving forward gently into a new life. Therefore, I would like to present here some of the many inconsistencies that I discovered in myself and in my male clients as we started that journey toward health. Take time to ponder them as you read through this section.

Isolate When We're Lonely

Think about this. Isolate when we're lonely? It doesn't make any sense. Mr. Spock or Commander Data from the Starship Enterprise would be baffled. I can hear either of them saying, "But, Captain, why would a human want to isolate if he was lonely? Logic would dictate that a lonely man would want to seek the company of his fellows. I don't understand." It doesn't make sense but we men aren't always as logical as we would like to believe. The truth is that our fear of getting close to others, especially other men, is what over-rides the logic here. The way to get past it is to find other men who are willing to admit their fear with you. The loneliness will then take care of itself.

Drink A Lot Of Alcohol To Feel Close

Alcohol is known to reduce our inhibitions, so it would seem logical to drink alcohol if you want to get closer to others. But there's a hitch here. Interactions between people who are high on something aren't very real. Anyone who has had an evening of "deep emotional intimacy" while high will attest to that if they can be honest. Intimacy while high is a sham and a fraud. It feels good while it's happening but it feels scary, shameful, icky and unreal the next day. The other problem is that people who rely on chemicals for their intimacy can only be intimate when they're high, which seems pretty darned limited if you ask me. *Healthy men have closeness without chemicals.*

Use Chemicals To Feel Better

Same problem. You may feel better in the moment, but you won't feel better when the chemical wears off. And if you use this strategy a lot, you become an addict. Then your life will start to collapse all around you and you'll really feel bad. It isn't very logical.

Hurt Those We Love

I write more about this in another chapter, but think about how illogical we get about those we "love." I put love in quotes because when we are on a regular regimen of hurting those we love, it isn't really love at all — it's dependency. We would be more logical if we just called a spade a spade here and said, "We tend to hurt those on whom we are pathologically dependent." There, that's logical.

Intellectualize Our Feelings

That's a pretty confusing heading also. *Ideas* are things that are *thought*. *Feelings* are reactions that are *felt*. You can't think a feeling and you can't feel a thought. The two affect each other back and forth, which is why cognitive-restructuring therapies are so effective. In other words, I can talk myself into being more depressed or more frightened than I need be, and I can feel something so intensely that my thoughts come racing out of my brain. But if you're having trouble with expressing feelings, do the logical thing — feel your feelings instead of thinking about them.

Expect Others To Anticipate Our Needs And Then Punish Them When They Don't Deliver

Other people aren't mind readers, so there's no logic to this one either. Many men and women are fooled into believing that they should be mind readers when they are growing up in their families. They never learn to ask for what they need, or when they ask, they never get it. So they quit asking or informing us about what they need. But it just isn't fair or logical to operate this way. It is even more unfair and illogical to punish others for not being able to do the impossible.

Control Those We Love

I know this sounds like a broken record, but this is also a gross contradiction in terms. Trite as it may sound, love is simply a gift. A gift is freely given. There can't be any strings attached. Control isn't about love, it's about fear and domination, which are also contradictions of love. Thus the decision we must make is whether we want to love someone or whether we want to control them. Each time we reach out to someone or interact with them, we must make this choice. The more mature our love, the more we are able to reach out with no need to control.

Lose Ourselves In Love

You guessed it! Another contradiction! It isn't possible to love another in a grown-up way unless we do it from a position of self-wholeness. To say "I'm lost in love" would be a lot more logical if we were to say, "My identity wasn't very clear when I got involved in this relationship. I'm trying to fuse with my lover and it isn't working. I don't feel love. I feel terrified, desperate, addictive, controlling and lost. Help!" In other words, I'm not "lost in love." I'm lost in addictiveness.

Lie To Protect Others From Our Dishonesty

Another contradiction in terms. Did I lie about an affair to protect someone else? Or was the lie done to protect myself from having to grow up and be man? In our close relationships, others feel what's going on whether we admit it or not, so that our lies actually hurt more than what we are lying about. Furthermore, when we lie to "protect others," we rob them of their dignity. By presenting them with an "untrue reality," we keep them from having the option to choose something else. If I own up to my affair, you may decide that you don't want to stay with me. You may be stronger than I am and able to choose being alone over being in an unfaithful relationship. By lying, I hold all the cards. I get to go out, have a fling and then come home to the safety and warmth of my home. But I also do something else: I become a little boy instead of a man. And then *none* of my relationships can be healthy.

Need Fathering But Push All Men Away

It is hard to trust people who are more powerful when we have been hurt growing up. And yet if we don't take the risk to find mentors and father-figures, we'll never get the father-healing that we need. In the seminars that I give around the U.S., I talk about the top 5% of the people on the planet who came from extremely healthy families, and everyone laughs and asks, "But where are they?" Think about it. Five percent of 250 million people is 12.5 million! There are a lot of healthy people out there, and the only way to find them is to keep risking. It's kind of like sales. You have to knock on a lot of doors before you make a sale, but when you do, it's worth it.

Keep trying. If your efforts in your daily world don't work, then go to a men's Co-dependents Anonymous meeting or Adult Children of Alcoholics meeting. If that isn't safe enough, then get in a men's therapy group. If the meeting or group you try the first time doesn't feel right, then try another. If after trying numerous groups you still feel as if you hate everything about them then entertain the thought that the problem might be about your own resistance and pain rather than just about the groups.

Demand A Grown-up Woman Without Growing Up

If you read our first book, you are aware of the "cup analogy" that we use. Someone with a full cup is not going to get into an ongoing relationship with a person whose cup is empty. We choose friends and partners who are approximately equal to us in emotional growth and maturity. You cannot latch onto a healthy woman in the hopes that she will fill you up. It does not happen this way. The other problem here is that many men choose "impossible women" with whom to fall in love, instead of gradually getting healthy and dating along the way until ready to commit to a clear strong relationship. By picking the "impossible woman," we are announcing to the world that we don't want to grow up, that we want to be unfulfilled in love (the healthy woman will never go for us) and that we are too stubborn and scared to admit who we really are and where we are in our growth. I stayed little for a long time because I was too ashamed and too afraid to admit that I was little.

Blame Everyone Else For My Problems

Dan Burrows and Eileen Middleton, directors of our Lifeworks Clinic in Iowa, have an all-time favorite quote they heard from a client years ago. In the midst of a fairly intense session, he blurted out, "But I can't recover from my co-dependency! No one will let me!" Linda and I hear variations on this theme all the time in our private practices, too. Look at the heading of this section. How can my problems be due to everyone else? Surely it is possible that I am being persecuted. But in truth, one of the key features of an unrecovering addict is that he blames everyone else for his problems.

Men blame the women in their lives for all sorts of things, from their business failures and their alcoholism to their poor relationships with their children. I once knew a man who flew into town every four to six weeks to see his children for an hour or so and wasn't present to them when he was there, but blamed the kids and his wife for their estrangement! Oh, the excuses we weave to explain the problems we have. In addiction circles this kind of thinking is called *delusional*. We all have some of it. Look at how illogical it really is. Then you can change it.

Act Tough When We Need To Be Vulnerable

Everyone needs defenses. Without them we would be opened up to too many dangers in life all at once. Everyone needs to find safe places in life where they can let down their defenses, too. Without our vulnerability, we would not be capable of intimacy. True, there are times when the right thing to do is to be tough. But many people act tough when the very thing they need to do is to be vulnerable. It's a risk, I'll grant you that. If I let you know that you're hurting me, you may use that against me. But if I don't let you know, you may never stop, so when I finally leave the relationship, you won't know why.

* * *

There are many more "logical" things we do that are actually illogical. *Think* about it. Then *feel* it. Something may just change for you today.

2

FATHERS AND HEROES

What a father says to his children is not heard by the world, but it will be heard by posterity.

Jean Paul Richter
Levana (1807)

4

Some Things I Learned From My Dad

AN INTRODUCTION TO FATHERING

When I was working on my Ph.D. in psychology in 1970, I was fascinated by a story in one of the voluminous textbooks that we had to read. I believe it was an edited anthology of articles on personality development, with a chapter on independence or autonomy. The author was making a point about the development of independence and personal mastery by telling a subtle powerful story about a Native American boy.

The boy was in a hut with some of the tribal elders, including the chief. A very heavy solid wood door closed off the entrance to the hut and the little boy wanted to go outside. He was about five or six and the door was very heavy and solidly

33

closed against the doorframe. The little boy went to the door and began to tug on the handle, but the door wouldn't budge. He tugged and tugged and tugged. Then he turned and looked back at the tribal elders, who looked directly at him with silent, serious, expressionless faces. The boy resumed his important work of trying to get the door open. He tugged and grunted and tugged some more.

For what seemed to be an eternity, that little boy worked at getting the door open, periodically looking back plaintively at the elders, who in turn simply looked on with detached interest. At last the little boy budged the door open. He turned around slowly to see the reaction of his elders. The chief looked down at the little boy with a very dignified expression and nodded in silent approval. The little boy beamed then went outside.

What a marvelous story! It is not only about the fostering of autonomy and independence, it is a story about the subtlety of fathering, about how many parents spoil their children while robbing them of the satisfaction of facing challenges on their own. This Native American boy was allowed to face his challenge alone, and he therefore got to take the credit for getting the door open, which gave him a feeling of self-sufficiency. He was one step closer to being a man.

Fathering is such a nebulous term. What is it that fathers are supposed to give to sons? In our culture, men have become so removed from their father role that most of us do indeed have a deep Father Wound to heal. Because fathers are more detached and absent from their children, sons have a very hard time forming bonds of identification with their fathers. This is even more of a problem now that many men are engaged in such abstract work. Dad leaves home in the morning in a business suit and returns home in the evening with a copy of the *Wall Street Journal* that he has been reading on the train. Where has he been? Who has he seen? What has he done all day? We don't know. So we lose something we might have had if Dad were a farmer, an auto mechanic in a nearby shop or a blacksmith.

While some of us may have a clear idea of what Dad does for a living, if our Dad is emotionally shut down and uninvolved in our lives while he's away from his work, we will suffer the same Father Wound nonetheless. If our fathers didn't get the fathering that they needed when they were boys, how on earth will they know what to do with us when we come into the world? They won't. Unless they get a lot of help somewhere.

WHAT IS FATHERING?

One way that I have heard fathering described is to say it is what men give to each other, while mothering is what women give to each other. This implies that women can't give fathering to their children, and with this I agree. A woman can teach a boy how to rebuild a carburetor, but it won't be fathering that she's giving him because she's not a man. That's simple enough to understand, I think. But the important question is, what is good fathering? I mean, let's face it. By his own example, a father can teach his son to be manipulative, ruthless, deceitful, cruel and dishonest with women, insensitive, irresponsible, addictive or help-less, powerless, ashamed, fearful, emotionally shut down and constantly apologetic. But what kind of fathering would that be? Not very good. Fathering may be what men give to each other, but it has to be more than that too.

I remember a psychologist who gave a talk back in the late 1970s when the women's/men's liberation movement was still pretty strong. He took a big risk in my estima-tion, because he suggested that one of the father's major roles was to help to separate the child from the mother as the child entered adolescence. This was a very unpopular idea back then as it might still be. But I think that he was right, in a subtle way, even in today's dual-career family. Somehow that male-biological-cultural tendency toward separateness is still there and it is still an important con-tributor to child development.

This notion is beautifully acknowledged by Robert Bly in his use of the Iron John tale, in which a man's job is to provide a rite of initiation for a boy who is ready to enter manhood.

WHAT I LEARNED FROM MY FATHER

But fathering is more than this, too. To help describe how fathering works, I will begin by telling you a little bit about my father. My father was a wonderful man in many ways: generous, concerned about our welfare in overt ways, an excellent provider, enthusiastic, optimistic, he would give the shirt off his back to help us or one of our friends who was in trouble. Eventually he was very successful in his career after a period of being somewhat of a "hell-raiser," so he eventually became a role model for how to operate in the world of work and how to get along with others without being a victim.

After quitting high school in his senior year because of an argument with an English teacher, he moved to San Francisco in the 1930s, met my mother, worked during the day while attending law school at night and passed the California bar exam. He never went to college. He found a mentor who took him in and taught him the ropes, and eventually he went out on his own. From that point on, he always took in young attorneys, gave them business and taught them the ropes. He was almost compulsively honest in his business dealings, too.

Once when he completed a two-year negotiation with a large group of corporate attorneys in New York City, they took him aside and said, "Mr. Friel, you're the most honest, honorable attorney with whom we have ever dealt."

My father had a zest for life and a sense of humor that was infectious. He had the constitution of a horse, too. This helps explain how he managed to run his law practice, coach Little League baseball, learn to water ski with his kids when he was in his 60s, spend dinner time every night sharing his day with my mother, then drink vast amounts of whiskey each night. Each morning he would be up bright and early, ready to face the day with the same enthusiasm and optimism of the day before. This was his regimen on and off for years.

You see, my father was a great human being in many ways. But he was also an alcoholic. Beneath his alcoholism and denial there was also a lot of pain, darkness and fear that came spilling out into our family system. A lot of that pain was from the emotional abuse he endured from his father who belittled him and told him throughout his life that he would "never amount to anything," which he set out to prove wrong.

As a survivor of abuse, he did what all survivors do — he married another survivor of abuse and then the two of them passed it on to their children. I believe that a lot of us get confused about what it means to be a man or a woman. We look at our fathers and mothers and we say, "*That* didn't work," and we try something different which doesn't work either. Then we really feel confused. That's one of the tragedies of family system re-enactment. In trying to improve, we often go to the other extreme and create a different but equal kind of dysfunction.

So I also saw another side of my father. In my own recovery work, it took me years to overcome my fear of being weak and vulnerable — a fear that kept me from crying between the ages of 7 and 28. Dad was terrified of his vulnerability. At first it made me terrified and ashamed of mine. Then, as I worked that through, it simply left me sad that he was so emotionally disabled. I am glad that he was able to die with dignity in his own home as he wanted to but I am sad that he did not have the recovery opportunities that I have had.

Dad had a tremendous amount of shame in general, too, which kept him from admitting his alcoholism. During my struggle with whether or not I should join Alcoholics Anonymous, I went to Dad and said, "Dad, I think I'm an alcoholic. I think I'm going to join AA. And I think you're an alcoholic, too." He tried. I could see that he tried to be understanding and compassionate and caring and fatherly, but he couldn't handle the reality and the shame. He replied, "No, I'm not an alcoholic, John. And don't let anyone know you're in AA. I had a colleague once who was in AA and it ruined his career." However, what he hadn't known was that his colleague had ruined his career because he had started drinking again.

All I had really needed him to say was, "John, do what you need to do. I'll support you." Or even more powerful might have been a wise and dignified nod of approval, like the Chief gave to the little boy who had just opened the door. That would have been wonderful. After all, I had just opened a huge, heavy door.

One of the last things that I forgave my father and mother for was that they did not put me into treatment for alcoholism when I was 19 or 20 years old. It was an act of profound neglect on my parents' part to let me and my friends drink vast amounts of alcohol in our house while they sat upstairs and watched television. It took me a long time to figure out that in a very real sense, I had been sacrificed to cover up their shame. Why? Because to send me to treatment would have exposed their alcoholism. So it all just stayed "secret."

I re-enacted a similar dynamic in my later life with an associate who encouraged me to sneak and hide my smoking from our staff. Although he preached the evils of smoking, he never once expressed his concern about mine. I should have been intervened upon about my smoking or at the very least, not encouraged to sneak. Sneaking is about addictive shame, and addictive shame helps to keep us addicted. I quit a few days after ending my relationship with this associate, and I pray every day that I don't start again.

When I found my recovery among a group of people who were willing to admit their shame and fear, as well as their anger and joy, I discovered I could be a true human being with feelings and strengths and weaknesses. I also discovered there were heroes all around me whom I had never seen before because I hadn't been open to seeing them. As I began to identify with people in recovery, I came to the painful realization that Dad had some other faults, too. I knew these already, but I didn't *know* them. What I realized was that Dad had a very angry, untrusting side to him, which made him very opinionated and judgmental of others.

I noticed that he had a lot of associates and acquaintances, but that he lacked any true friends with whom he could be safely vulnerable. His opinions were so strong and rigid, I unconsciously began to believe there was only one right way to do things — that mere matters of individual preference were really powerful statements of one's intelligence and worth.

"You like THAT!" became a regular part of my phraseology and thinking. If you didn't wash your clothes with Tide, like vanilla ice cream, go to movies only in the evening, run instead of walk for your exercise, vote Democratic, like Hawaii and enjoy science, math and reading, well then, there was something wrong with you!

Sometimes I saw my father's fear of his own vulnerability turn into a vicious contempt for others' vulnerability. I carried this feeling myself for many years and didn't surrender it completely until I hit bottom with my own alcoholism. Sometimes I saw my father turn his contempt for vulnerability against his loved ones, which made me feel angry, disgusted, sad and ashamed of being a Friel. It was one of the most painful and important parts of my own recovery from abuse to admit to myself and others that I had unconsciously picked up some of this contempt and was acting it out in my own life.

It was even more important when I decided to change this behavior in myself, because it is so easy to see and admit things and intellectually understand them, but so hard to actually change them.

Perhaps the most confusing and difficult realization is that while my father was honest and honorable in the overt world, he had a very hard time being honest and honorable in the covert world of feelings and relationships. This was so confusing because one wouldn't think that a person could be so split in two. But in truth, we do it all the time. Within the same day or the same hour, I could see him be caring and concerned about a poor client or friend of ours in the community, then see him be clumsily and hurtfully oblivious to the emotional goings-on of a friend or family member. I watched him care deeply about his children then turn around and wound us deeply with his abruptness or emotional ineptitude. It was all confusing to me for many years.

What of his incredibly strong physical constitution? I watched my father have a mild stroke which left his face temporarily paralyzed and his speech mildly slurred. Then I saw him go into court that same day, before going to a doctor, to present his case.

Years later he suffered a massive stroke and went into a coma for two weeks. We all said our goodbyes and prepared for his death. The doctors said that we would have to decide soon when to take him off life support, and we said we knew that. We told the doctor the story of his going into court after his mild stroke, we described what a strong character he was, and we said, "Let's wait a few more days." The next day he came out of the coma and went on to live another seven years.

For a long time afterwards, I took that tale to mean that Friels were invincible. It was only in my recovery that I awoke to the painful truth that he never would have had the stroke in the first place had he not smoked and drank all of his adult life. It took me a long time to untangle the messages in that tale, believe me.

AM I LIKE MY DAD?

My father was a man of painful contrasts. Many fathers are, as are many mothers. So what did this mean for me? There was a part of me that wanted to be like Dad because he was my dad. That's how this all works. There was another part of me that didn't want to be like Dad at all, because he was insensitive, even cruel at times, and because he was so afraid, ashamed and addicted. "I'm going to do just the opposite," I told myself. That's exactly what I tried to do. There's a snag here, though, because the opposite of sick is sick! The opposite of "uncaring and unfeeling" is to wallow in emotions and care so much that we lose ourselves in the process. The opposite of "cruel" is to be a victim. The opposite of being afraid of one's vulnerability is to wear it like a mantle of false martyrdom. The opposite of shame about one's vulnerability is to become holier than thou, moralistic and falsely proud of one's weaknesses so that we use this as an excuse not to become powerful. The opposite of "too detached" is "too enmeshed."

Who did I become? I became a boy in man's clothing who had a huge internal battle going on between the good parts of my parents and the unhealthy parts of my parents. This battle was even more highlighted because I am a third child, and third children tend to take on more of the marital relationship.

Did I become like the "bad" parts of Dad even though I tried to be the exact opposite? You bet I did! I became an alcoholic just like Dad. I carried his fear of vulnerability, fear of tears and shame. I carried his rigid judgments about people who were "different." He was a great debater and arguer, so I got really good at arguing and debating, which allowed me to stay even further away from emotional realities and gave me even more skills in denying my addictiveness and other dysfunctions.

We psychotherapists know that some of the hardest clients to deal with are the highly defensive, intellectualized ones who have a reason for everything, a comeback and a defense or justification. I have a hunch that my father believed that if he thought it, it was real. Unfortunately, much of what we think is just in our heads — it isn't real at all. I picked this one up in a big way. I *thought* for a long time that I was not alcoholic. I *thought* for a long time that I was a sensitive, gentle, caring, liberal, humanistic kind of guy who never judged anyone. I was in for some surprises.

Do you know what else happened? When I finally did some big, scary pieces of therapy work around how I was just like Dad in ways I had tried not to be, then I could embrace the parts of Dad that were truly honorable. In other words, instead of running away from the "Father

pain" inside me, I had to run toward it. As I admitted the
frightening flaws I had received from Dad, I was also able
to embrace, develop and celebrate Dad's true strengths
and virtues. It is difficult to emphasize enough how important this is to our healing as men. And so I'll state it
again . . .

*We are like Dad. We are like the "bad" parts of Dad, too.
Until we admit and embrace the "bad" parts of Dad, we
can't change those parts in ourselves. Until we admit those
parts, we will have a very hard time fully developing the good
parts in ourselves that we picked up from Dad.*

SOME GOOD THINGS

I will never forget the childlike wonder, awe and respect
that my father had for the Constitution of the United
States. He told me once about his visit to the U.S. Supreme
Court. He stood before the empty bench almost in tears
as he heard the voices of Justices, the Chief Justice and
lawyers pleading their cases and forming opinions that
have shaped our nation, for better or worse, over the past
200 years. I won't forget his infectious sense of humor or
his ability to compete in games and sports with a sense of
fairness and fair-play that was wondrous to behold. Somehow he was able to give his all in such competition without
worrying about the final outcome. It actually didn't matter
if he won or lost, but how he played the game that mat-
tered. That sounds trite, I realize, except for one thing.
He really *lived* it rather than talking about it.

I won't forget his boundless energy and enthusiasm for
life. I won't forget the one time I saw him cry, when he
was moving out of our home for a temporary separation
from my mother when we were little kids. I won't forget
his willingness to accept his kids' criticisms of some of his
less shameful faults. I won't forget his unique mix of
dedicated, thorough competence at work coupled with a
rather mistake-ridden impulsiveness when away from his
work. He was a master gardener and when he died, he

left a yard filled with fruit trees, pine trees, bird-feeders and hundreds of birds that visited each day.

I will always remember the times he took me to his office in the San Francisco financial district when I was very young. He would be finishing up a project on a Saturday morning, and I would go with him and wax the bindings of his old law books, play with the adding machine, fool with the telephone and look out at all of the cars on the street far down below. He went out of his way to take me to work with him so that I could see him in the courtroom, too, which gave me a concrete picture of what he did for a living. I will always appreciate his love of movies, which is something that I like, too. He taught me to care for those around me, especially my family.

One of the great gifts that came to me as I demythologized my father and our relationship was my career. Until that time, I was a Ph.D. psychologist without a life, a plan or a career. I was miserable and floundering. I left psychology for almost two years. I hated it. Then I embraced my alcoholism. I did two years of painful anger and grief work around my father and mother. For years, I had protected them so much that I couldn't even admit that they were addicts, but now I hated them for a time. I sobbed to the depth of my soul. I went in and out of a dark hole from which I wondered whether I would ever return.

Slowly, I began to heal from the inside out. It was like coming out of a terrible, violent storm into a bright sunny warm mountain meadow. Then my career path unfolded to me, and I knew that I finally had somewhere to go. It was around that same time that I met Linda. For the first time in my life, *I felt my life*. I am now grateful to my father and mother for the good things that they gave me. But I no longer pretend that I was not deeply hurt by the bad things that they gave me. I am grateful, that's all.

Heroes

The three men I admire most,
The Father, Son and the
Holy Ghost,
They caught the last train
for the coast,
The day the music died.

Don McLean
American Pie

ASK YOURSELF ABOUT YOUR HEROES

Many people complain that we have a shortage of true heroes these days. In some ways I agree with the statement, but with qualifications. I think there *are* heroes around, but they don't always get the most media attention. This fact makes it hard for kids to find strong healthy role models. But it goes much deeper than that.

Who are the three men that *you* admire most? When a boy doesn't have a father who is present in his life, he has a hard time looking up to any heroes. Think about the phrase, "look up to." Imagine a little boy looking up to see his tall father there, but no one is there. Or when the little boy looks up into the "heavens" to see his father standing tall above him, the father looks down and slaps him, snaps at him, makes fun of him or just goes away out of his own fear.

Now imagine that same boy a little older. He struggles to look up to the men around him, but now he isn't sure how to do it. One day he is mistrustful of men and believes that men are out to hurt him in some way. The next day he goes to the other extreme and builds a fantasy relationship with his newest "hero," only to be disappointed later when he discovers that his hero is a human being, has faults and isn't a perfect substitute Dad.

The boy becomes an adolescent. Now his hunger for a hero is even stronger. But he has a deep wound. So he finds heroes who can help him express his hurt and outrage. In the '60s there were a lot of them around.

I encourage you to take an interested yet detached look at the heroes you found at various stages in your life — meander around your life for a few weeks, answer the questions below and then discuss them with your friends, loved ones, therapist or recovery group.

1. Who did/do I admire and look up to?
2. Was/is there anyone?
3. If not, how did/does that feel?
4. If so, who were/are they?
5. And how did/does that feel?
6. Did you have different heroes at different stages in your life?
7. If so, was there a pattern to the men you admired?
8. Which of the heroes would you now be embarrassed to admit you had?
9. Is there anyone you admire today?
10. Would you feel comfortable telling others about your present heroes?
11. Step back a little from the men you now admire. Look at them objectively. What traits do they possess? What kind of men are they?
12. What does it say about you to have such heroes?

13. How do your feelings change when you find out painful truths about a man whom you admire?
14. After admiring someone, have you had to put him on your Fallen Heroes List because the truth about him was just too dysfunctional to ignore any longer?
15. How did it feel to put these men on that List?

Who we pick as heroes says a lot about us. By way of example, let me share with you some of the men I have admired in my life. Maybe my list will help you start a list of your own.

SOME MEN I HAVE ADMIRED IN MY TIME

Birth Through Eighth Grade

As I look back over my list of role models, there is a very clear progression. There is a pattern to my heroes. It isn't always a tidy pattern, but there are meaningful trends. For starters, I looked up to my father and my older brother. They were the first "male higher powers" in my life. I clearly remember the exuberance with which my father would tell the story about my staring into our neighbors' swimming pool while my brother and sister were swimming, and then simply falling into the pool. I was apparently entranced by the water, but sank to the bottom without a struggle. My brother saw me, dived into the pool, grabbed me and pulled me out, saving my life. When we were children, my father would tell that story over and over, praising my brother for his quick response and laughing good-naturedly about my relaxed approach to drowning.

I remember my father and brother excitedly watching the Friday Night Fights on our first black and white television set. I wasn't old enough to enjoy boxing or wasn't sportsminded enough because I always got bored. I couldn't wait for the commercials to come on so that I could watch The Gillette parrot flap around the screen, yelling "Look sharp! Feel sharp! Be sharp!"

My older brother was a typical older brother in an alcoholic family back then or maybe he was just a typical older brother. Most of the time he was pretty nice to me and sometimes he would tease me. But some of the time he would try to tell me what to do, what to think and boss me around — typical older brother stuff.

Once I got into grammar school, I admired many of the heroes that school children learn about. I thought George Washington was pretty neat. I bought the myth about the cherry tree, too. We learned Abraham Lincoln single-handedly freed the slaves and saved the Union from permanent ruin. I remember shuddering at the mere thought of the Union breaking up into two countries. Whatever would have happened to us? Would the world have stopped rotating on its axis?

I wondered in amazement at the way America's history had turned out so perfectly. It fit exactly into the value and meaning system of my teachers, my family and everyone else. White men were good. Indians were bad. That's why Indians became alcoholic and got stuck on reservations. It's where they belonged, I surmised shallowly. If you tried to tell me otherwise back then, I would have argued you into a corner.

Benjamin Franklin was a fine upstanding man who was practical, inventive, politically astute and very moralistic. When I was in the fourth grade, I never would have believed that he fathered illegitimate children. The Confederate Army was bad, the Union Army was good. The United States of America single-handedly won World War II despite the ineptitude of our allies. The Russians were evil. Communists were worse than evil. And Jesus Christ? Well, He was God. I knew that. What I didn't understand at the age of four was why He didn't just destroy His enemies and prevent His painful crucifixion right then and there, rather than going through with it. He was God. I looked up to Him. But that "going through with it" stuff really confused me.

I had a couple of sports heroes also. Living in the San Francisco Bay Area, I thought Willie Mays was the cat's meow. I doubt if there will ever be an outfielder as great as he was. He was the "Say-Hey Kid," and even people who knew nothing about baseball loved Willie. Yes, I admired Mickey Mantle, too, even though he played for the Yankees. Then there were Y.A. Tittle, Johnny Unitas and scores more.

I was also fortunate back in the early '50s to have had a couple of male grammar school teachers, which was rare back then. I liked that a lot. I had one teacher in particular who taught seventh grade. He was likeable, he liked us, and best of all, he challenged the heck out of us. Every once in a while he would say just one little thing that would be so startling, unique and uncomfortable that we would never forget it. Remember, that was the era of Walt Disney, the Mickey Mouse Club and the suburban American dream. Lo and behold, one day out of the blue, with brashness and nerve unheard of in Marin County, California, this teacher said, "I'm not so sure that everything about Disney is good."

Then he just went on talking as if he hadn't said the most iconoclastic heretical crazy thing of his entire life. Can you believe it? Disney not good? That one statement literally made me think for years. It was simply wonderful. A school teacher who got kids to think. Incredible!

High School Years

During high school I began to get very confused about who I was and who I should be like. Having alcoholic parents made it even worse. I had converted to Catholicism at age 14 because my older sister and brother had, so I was really caught up in trying to be like saints and angels and martyrs and holy men. There were also a couple of priests I really liked, too. One was an alcoholic biology teacher. Another was a religion and Latin teacher who was pretty strict, but also had a gentle, soft, intellectually bright quality about him that made sitting through Catholic high school somewhat reasonable. Another was an English teacher who had the gall to try to teach us how to write. In the words of Agent Cooper from ABC's *Twin Peaks*, he did a "damned fine" job of it, too!

I will always value one history teacher I had. He was a thin fragile-looking man. I think he wore a lot of tweed. He was working on his Ph.D. in history and loved history. He walked into that classroom filled with borderline juvenile delinquents and rabble-rousers. We took one look at him and assumed that he would be an easy mark for our torment. Instead that shy man put every one of us in a trance with his love of history. It was truly wondrous to behold. Even the most apathetic among us got excited about history. He made history come alive by having us read original documents and articles that told the truth about all of the myths we had learned in grammar school.

We discovered George Washington's cutting down a cherry tree was a story fabricated by Parson Weems as part of a Washington's Birthday celebration. Ben Franklin was a great man, *and* he fathered illegitimate children. FDR had a mistress for years. Lincoln suffered from clinical depression. And the Civil War was about economics more than it was about slavery.

The history teacher from the previous year had required us to memorize 200 dates for our final examination. Then this new guy waltzes in and announces "Dates are the love of a secondhand scholar!" He spent the rest of the year showing us why. He *educated us*, in the true sense of the word. He led us out of the darkness and we loved it. I had always hated history prior to that class, but from then on, I loved it. We learned trends, dynamics, movements, politics and the "whys" and "wherefores." We talked about the "what ifs," and the "maybes." He led us out of the darkness of absolute black-and-white thinking.

Then one day he was late coming back from lunch. He walked into our classroom, a few tears running down his cheeks, his voice shaking, hand trembling and face pale white. He looked down at us compassionately and announced that President Kennedy had been shot.

Everything changed after that. Vietnam escalated. My friends and I started to experiment with marijuana and alcohol. We listened to Bob Dylan records when no one had even heard of the guy. A lot of people thought we were weird. We wrote poetry. A couple of my friends wrote good poetry that was recognized by the likes of Allen Ginsberg and Lawrence Ferlinghetti. One even published with City Lights Books when he was still in high school.

We discovered a place called the Fillmore Auditorium. I remember going there in the early days when there might be only a hundred people listening to The Jefferson Airplane or the Grateful Dead. My father was extremely worried about that because the Fillmore was in a poor part of San Francisco. My going there wasn't just a good way to bond with my peers. It was a great way to rebel against what I perceived to be the fearfulness and prudishness of my parents.

I found a bushel full of new heroes to admire. There were Bob Dylan, the poet-troubador of an angry generation, Jimi Hendrix, Jerry Garcia, Pete Townshend, James Baldwin, Malcolm X, Allen Ginsberg and scores of other emerging rock stars, political activists, poets, outlaws and Hell's Angels with whom to bond. It was especially confusing because many of these people represented legitimate complaints about society and the family, even though for many of us they also provided an approved backdrop for acting out our family pain.

Many of these people became what I call my *Dark Heroes*. My identification with them was actually coming out of my own painful, addictive childhood. By their example and their fame, they gave me permission to do all kinds of self-destructive things like drinking, smoking and overworking.

I see the same thing happening for Oliver Stone right now in 1991. When I read David Breskin's interview with him in *Rolling Stone* magazine, what I saw was the brilliant and talented man who made one of my favorite films *Platoon*. What I also saw was a man who is not just "stuck in the '60s," but still trying to glorify sexual addiction and alcoholism and appears to be in a lot of pain as a result.

Oliver Stone's discomforting denial is apparent in his statement about Jim Morrison: "Meanness? Abusive? The only abusiveness I know of — from all the witnesses — was when he was drinking." If Morrison drank one-tenth of what we saw him drink in Stone's film, then he was a big time offender and a big time alcoholic.

I don't always agree with conservative social critic George Will, but I have to admit that his analysis of the '60s in his critique of Stone's film, *The Doors*, was pretty compelling. He said that, "Morrison, an icon of the drug culture, ingested his share of drugs but was basically a drunk . . . The central myth of the '60s was that the wretched excess was really a serious quest for new values."

If you're still stuck in the '60s, especially in terms of being bonded with addicts, see *The Doors*, then read Will's essay. I suspect it will make you think. In my recovery journey I have discovered that euphoria and expanded consciousness can come from *living every day* rather than drugs.

I was in high school from 1961 to 1965 and had some other heroes, too. There was John F. Kennedy, a dashing, charming, witty, tough young president who challenged his nation to put a man on the moon before the end of the '60s and stared down Krushchev during the Cuban Missile Crisis.

Then there was his brother, Bobby, who stood up to George Wallace and Lester Maddox in the fight for civil rights in the South. I was naive about politics then, as was most of the nation. I had the "white knight on the white horse" mentality about all of this. The Kennedys were good. The South was bad. Jimmy Hoffa was bad. Bobby Kennedy was going to slay the dragon. I admired Martin Luther King, Jr. He galvanized an entire nation of squabbling factions by his life-threatening marches and highly moral civil disobedience. I choked back the tears as I listened to his speeches and followed his progress on television.

College And Graduate School Years

Then I went to college. While at the University of San Francisco I found several men I could look up to. There were a couple of Jesuit priests I admired for their philosophical and theological brilliance and because they challenged me to think in new ways. There was a literature professor whose infectious love of literature, especially 20th century American novels, rubbed off on me and to whom I am eternally grateful. And several psychology professors helped me develop a love of psychology *and* scientific inquiry which remains with me today.

During graduate school I was fortunate to have some professors who were not abusive, which I still find to be a rarity based on my clients' stories. I don't know if my professors realized how important it was to treat us humanely compared to how other graduate students were treated around the U.S. Compared to medical school faculty, they were downright saints. As a result, I felt a strong bond with a couple of my professors and felt as if I got a good deal of healthy guidance and fathering that I needed.

During these years I also began to get to know my brother-in-law, Bill McIntyre, who had married my sister when I was 14 years old. In my eyes, he was like a father figure for a long time while I was growing up and out of my adult child pain. He was a Marine Corps jet fighter pilot who had a heart and a soul, and I learned a lot of "guy things" from him on our many trips on the ocean, deep-sea fishing. He is a brother to me now, but I will always be grateful that he came into my life when he did. He is the kind of guy who is comfortable with being a man and comfortable with his sensitivity as well.

After School Was Over

With my Ph.D. in hand I entered the "real world" and discovered that my education was just beginning. It was then I faced what I described in earlier chapters of this book — my recovery from alcoholism and the damage I sustained growing up in an alcoholic home. For a while I continued to protect and admire a lot of the addicted heroes from my past — my Dark Heroes. But I also noticed a transformation taking place within.

I began to read about famous recovering people, including some of my heroes from the '60s and '70s who had sobered up and were leading healthier lives. From Dennis Wholey's *The Courage To Change,* I learned, for example, that Pete Townshend, the musical genius behind *The Who,* was clean, sober and publishing his own and others' written works. I noticed that my tolerance for active addicts became less and that my comfort level with recovering addicts became greater. Instead of always identifying with people who had made a mess of their lives, as I had, I found myself identifying with people who had turned their lives around and were making something magical out of the mess. Brilliant actor and director, Dennis Hopper, comes to mind here.

My sense of wonder and mystery about life that had become lost amidst all the emotional abuse of childhood began to return. I found myself drawn to people who had a sense of wonder and mystery about life, but weren't scary or crazy about it. It was rather like the wonder and magic of *Shoeless Joe,* W.P. Kinsella's novel upon which the film *Field of Dreams* was based. Life is still unpredictable for me today, but not in the destructive ways that it once was. I still have people I admire, but not the Dark Heroes I once had. I still admire my father, but I don't admire his alcoholism or his emotional child abuse of us.

CONTEMPORARY HEROES

For the past few months I have written names on little pieces of paper and inserted them into a manila folder titled "Contemporary Heroes." I thought that by doing this I would eventually be able to narrow a list to three or four men who mean the most to me now. But that hasn't happened. Each of the men in that folder has contributed something important to the world, each has his faults and each has his own arena of contribution. You might laugh at some or find them trivial, but I think it is very important to look at *all* of our role models, not just the ones who are "politically correct." Let's face it. Not everyone will become a Gandhi or a Mother Teresa. Perhaps the best thing would be to randomly sample from that list so that you can see what I mean, then you can begin your own list.

Nelson Mandela

I feel deeply honored to say that I share the same planet with a man like this. It is still difficult for me to comprehend the depth of commitment it must have taken to sacrifice 27 years of freedom for one's beliefs. I admire his breadth and depth of life experiences and the consummate dignity with which he has conducted his fight against *apartheid*. It is humbling for me to try to praise a man like this. My life has been so easy compared to his; my battles so small and so personal.

Mikhail Gorbachev/Eduard Shevardnadze

Gorbachev is under siege and may not even be in power by the time this book goes to print. I pray that he or other Soviet leaders do not revert back to a totalitarian government. I can only judge him based on what has happened up to the time of this writing. Based on that, I admire the awesome political survival skills that were necessary for him to become the leader of the Soviet Union. That he was able to orchestrate the fall of the Berlin Wall and the reunification of Germany is worthy of permanent historical merit regardless of how it all turns out. Gorbachev has demonstrated a toughness, a political deftness and a masterful understanding of the media far greater than most world leaders. If he turns into a totalitarian tyrant, I reserve the right to remove him from my list.

It is my understanding that years ago he and his trusted friend, Eduard Shevardnadze, who recently resigned as Soviet Foreign Minister, dreamed together of a Soviet Union that was free, open and productive. When Shevardnadze resigned, Gorbachev was visibly shaken, and in a recent television interview, Shevardnadze said that it was "agonizing and difficult for me. Maybe I let him down." But the interests of the people were more important. Of his friend, Gorbachev, he said, "A man who was not courageous could not have started *perestroika.*" They have both been enormously courageous, and I hope that his friend can get through his current crises with his dignity intact and with the integrity of his people intact as well.

Ron Kovic

He waited patiently for years, hoping to get his story out so that thousands of Vietnam War Veterans could finally heal. His waiting finally paid off when he and Oliver Stone put together *Born On The Fourth Of July.* You may not all agree with his opposition to our war with Iraq, but I challenge you to read his story or see the film and remain unimpressed. His courage, determination and honesty of feelings throughout his Vietnam healing process are no less than inspiring.

Bill W. and Dr. Bob

Back in 1935 the founders of Alcoholics Anonymous put together something that has revolutionized life in America, when all the odds said that they should have died of alcoholism instead. No doubt with the help of their Higher Power, these two drunks concocted a system of living that was ridiculed until recently by many psychologists. Now most professionals are scrambling to get on the AA bandwagon because they can no longer stem the tide of recovery that is inundating the nation.

Bob Hope

When I was in college, Bob Hope represented everything an anti-war protester loved to hate. Like John Wayne, Bob Hope seemed to be pro-war, pro-establishment, anti-intellectual, anti-compassion . . . you name it. I don't know anything about him privately, but the public

Bob Hope appears to be a kind generous funny man whose humor can still bring people together instead of tearing them apart. As a young man, I liked Lenny Bruce, mind you. But I have a lot of respect for a man who has such a sterling and distinguished career as Bob Hope. He has earned my respect and admiration.

Jay Leno

And while we're on the subject of comedians, I can't go by without giving Leno his due. Everyone, male and female, liberal and conservative, seems to be able to respect and enjoy this man. He takes a lot of risks in his humor, which knocks everything and everyone from presidents to telephone companies. He makes people think. His personality is strong and forceful yet gentle and compassionate. He has strong opinions without being shaming and dogmatic. He seems to be a clean-living person who is honest and powerful.

David Halberstam

The Pulitzer Prize winning *New York Times* reporter who covered Vietnam and then later wrote *The Best And the Brightest*, which was one of the best, the brightest, scariest, most thorough and most brilliant historical investigations into the origins and dark political underpinnings of our involvement in Vietnam. I admire his impartiality, his wisdom, his incisive intelligence and the risks he took to write the book.

Giorgio Perlasca

Soon to be honored in the U.S. Holocaust Museum in Washington, D.C., this man singlehandedly saved between 5,000 and 10,000 Hungarian Jews from the Nazis, risking his own safety and his life. By the sheer strength of his powerful presence, and, I believe, the power of his convictions, he stood toe to toe with Adolf Eichmann at one point and stared him down to save two children from certain death. Upon his return to his native Italy after the war, Perlasca never once tried to capitalize on his good works, living a humble existence in obscurity until just recently. Again, this kind of quiet heroism, motivated by some powerful internal principle of selfless morality, is awe-inspiring to me. Most of us would be hard-pressed to approach this man's accomplishment, but his actions are an inspiration for us to begin to try.

Martin Luther King, Jr.

It would be easy to trivialize his accomplishments here, so I won't try. All I can say is that I am grateful for what he did for black and white people in America. I travel a lot and I get a feel for different parts of the country. Maybe I'm wrong, but it seems to me that the most integrated, most tolerant part of America today is the South, where Martin Luther King focused most of his work and had his greatest impact. We have such a long way to go in terms of accepting each other as people instead of as blacks or whites or Hispanics or Asians. The memory of Martin Luther King and his message can help us all break free of our terrible disease of self-hatred, which is what I believe causes prejudice in the first place.

In his novel about life in Jamaica, Anthony Winkler wrote, "We all owe life and love to one another. Every single one of us. Dat is de way God plan dis world to be, and dere is no escaping it."

John Steinbeck

As many of you are aware, he is one of my favorite authors. I will never forget what I first learned about his writing in a class I once took — that he used simple sentences and clear direct words to paint incredibly powerful pictures. He had a broad range of life experiences and a spiritual connection with humanity. His compassion for all of us touched me so deeply years ago that I was never the same. As both a psychologist and a person recovering from a painful childhood, I feel honored, respected, understood and touched by Steinbeck.

Jean Piaget

Swiss psychologist Jean Piaget had a profound impact on my understanding of human development. But I was also fascinated by the story of his life. When I first began to learn about his work, I was in graduate school and was unsure of where I was heading with my career. Piaget's work, thinking and life story prompted me to keep asking questions and trying to understand. His method of investigation — noticing everyday behavior of infants and children rather than doing dry laboratory experiments — taught me that there was more than one legitimate way to learn the truth.

Erik Erikson

He was the psychoanalyst who broke with Freud's thinking about sexuality and proposed a theory of human development that emphasized social awarenesses and life stages. He coined the term "identity crisis," and showed that who we become is very much imbedded in our culture. I have used his eight stages of development in just about everything I write or do clinically.

General Norman Schwarzkopf

Stormin' Norman? He prefers his other nickname, "The Bear." If you had a chance to see Barbara Walters' wonderful interview with him on March 15, 1991, you saw a man who was a competent, effective, strong, "typically male" kind of guy. You also saw a man who wept with great dignity and grace when asked about having to leave his family behind when he went off to the Persian Gulf War and wept again when asked about the families of his troops. He is a man who likes the opera and had pictures of family members all over his humble quarters in Saudi Arabia. He shared that he has been scared in every war that he has been in. And this tough, perhaps crusty, four-star general said right on national television that *a man who can't cry scares him.* By all accounts, he embodies a man who has both fierceness and tenderness.

Stephen Hawking

The jacket cover of his bestselling book which we all bought and few understood, *A Brief History Of Time: From The Big Bang To Black Holes,* says he "is widely regarded as the most brilliant theoretical physicist since Einstein." I am in awe of him because of what he sees, and because of what he has done despite his total physical disability from Lou Gehrig's disease. I am in awe of his persistence, his ability to continue with his work despite his incapacitation and the deeply spiritual nature of his relationship with the universe. I have an intuitive sense of what he sees, and seeing him as he is, trapped in a body but in no way trapped, gives me hope. I thank him for that every time I think of him, read about him or see him on television.

Michael Crichton

When I began teaching General Psychology, the other faculty were using his book, *The Terminal Man,* as required reading, which was a grand way to make physiological psychology come alive. I was impressed with Crichton's popular writing ability and the fact that he had risked quitting medicine to pursue his lifelong dream of writing. I was even more impressed when I read his book, *The Great Train Robbery,* and learned that he directed the film version starring Sean Connery. Recently I discovered his book, *Travels,* a courageous, self-revealing series of essays and thoughts about his own outer and inner travels. I recommend this book to everyone now, and I admire what he has done with his career. Whether he'll ever know it or not, Michael Crichton helped me to realize *my* dreams, too.

WHAT SHOULD I DO WITH MY HEROES?

After you make a list of some of the men you admire, it is important to consider what you can learn from them and how you can learn from them. These last two can be tricky because we all have a tendency to fantasize our heroes.

Let your heroes become real people. Pick someone you admire, write down the reasons you admire him then do some research at the library. Get some books and magazine articles about him. Read a lot about him. Be open to seeing his flaws as well as his strengths. Notice how you feel when you discover his flaws.

I recently read an in-depth story about a movie actor I once admired. The contrast between his real life and his screen image was so shocking that I have become soured on him altogether. Remember that all human beings are imperfect, and that if you can't find any heroes because none are perfect, that's an issue for you to resolve.

Don't make a god out of your hero. See if you can learn from that hero of yours rather than simply idolizing him. When we idolize someone, we attribute mystical powers to them where none exist. Albert Einstein wasn't a brilliant physicist but a god, we tell ourselves. I can worship him, but I can't be anything like him, because I'm not a god. I could never spend 27 years of my life in prison for a just cause, as Nelson Mandela did so I'll idealize him instead. I used to look at people I admired and say, "I'd like to be like them, but I never will." Now, I look at someone I admire and I say, "I can do some of that. His life challenges me to improve myself. But I'll never be him, and that's okay. I'm me." Perhaps Nelson Mandela's awe-inspiring commitment can help me to make some commitments in my life, on a smaller scale. Maybe Thomas Jefferson's marvelously broad range of interests and skills can spur me to expand my world. If Job was willing to endure incredible loss and pain as a test of his faith, maybe I can endure some of the pain I'm experiencing in my life right now. See how it works?

See how they got there. As you get to know your hero in more depth, look closely at how he got where he is today. So many of us forget that there is a long and often confusing process involved in achieving personal success. Young children look up to Martin Luther King, Jr. and think, "He was always a famous civil rights leader." They look at a successful author, scientist, plumber or entrepreneur and say, "He's so lucky. He's always been success-ful." Children are not capable of seeing the intermediate steps involved in getting from nowhere to somewhere in life. They just assume that it's always been that way. Many of us who grew up in dysfunctional homes see life as if we are still six years old.

Use your noticing skills to see the steps in between. One of the most important things a father can teach a son is the importance of starting at the beginning, learning the ropes all the way up, paying one's dues and only then being ready to take the reins. This is true if a dad is teaching his son to paint a house, write an essay or devel-op a friendship. The steps in between are what makes one successful in a career, in a love relationship and in life. Read lots of biographies. Notice how your heroes got to where they are today. See the steps. Then start taking steps of your own.

Know your limits and set realistic goals. Each of us has different abilities and different ability levels. I can admire John Steinbeck's writing now without beating myself up because I can't write as well as he does. I don't need to be John Steinbeck to be happy. I can admire Jesus Christ, Gandhi, Buddha, Abraham Lincoln or George Washington now without feeling inadequate. I can learn from them, but I also have my own genetic and environmental limits.

Find the everyday heroes around you. Above all, it is essen-tial that you find the everyday heroes in your life. If you don't have any right now, it is crucial that you begin to work on that. What do I mean by everyday heroes? I mean Dad or a Dad-Substitute. I mean Mentors. I mean male friends who can give you "Fathering" and "Brother-ing." Heroes in magazines, films and history books are important, but they can never take the place of flesh-and-blood people who guide us, nurture us, teach us, set limits for us and care for us.

As you journey through the history of your own he-roes, let your life speak to you in ways it hasn't before. Notice the feelings that arise as you are on the journey. Feel your way through it. Learn to see with your heart instead of your eyes. Face the shame, listen to what it tells you and learn from it. Hear the joy. Trust the awe. Respect the truth that your journey brings you. The people we admire say a lot about who we are. It takes courage and vision to look at ourselves and then share what we find with others in our tribe. Above all, it is worth it.

6

What Are Dads Good For?

A client of mine once said, "My father wasn't around much, so I never learned to deal with my anger." Another said, "I never saw Dad stand up for himself." Yet another said, "I never learned to follow through with anything that I did because my father never expected me to follow through."

In the mid-1970s men finally began to write about men, partially in reaction to women writing about men. People like Herb Goldberg and Warren Farrell hit the bestseller lists with their men's books. Today we have books like Robert Bly's *Iron John* and the sensitive and spiritual book on men's recovery, *Catching Fire: Men Coming Alive In Recovery* by family therapist Merle Fossum. Comedian and fellow Minnesotan Louie Anderson has written one of the most touching and healing books for Adult Children to date, which I also strongly recommend: *Dear Dad: Letters From An Adult Child.* (Former) *Psychology Today* editor, Sam Keen, also has written *Fire In The Belly* on men. Until the 1960s, developmental psychologists rarely even spoke of the role of fathers in raising children, let alone doing research on us.

In truth, dads are singularly important in men's lives. Why? Because dads are men. Where else will we learn how to be male? Moms can't teach us to be men because they aren't male. That's simple enough, isn't it? Dads are important because they are the men in our lives. When a dad cries, it's different than when a mom cries, for the simple reason that he's a dad.

Dads are good for a lot of things, although you wouldn't know it from television. If you look at men on television programs and commercials, you will see bumbling, emasculated, selfish, stupid, inept men who can't seem to do anything right. They always seem to be married to, involved with or being constantly rescued by women who tolerate their men as charming but naughty children. Or these men and women are just bland connect-the-dots caricatures drawn from the latest self-help book. Contrary to these false television images, many *real* fathers are strong, clear, honorable, caring and loving with their sons without being emasculated *or* emasculating.

I see a lot of good fathers out there. Therefore, what I would like to do is tell you what I believe are some of the important things we can learn from our dads, if they are available to us. Please note that if you didn't have a dad available to you, you can learn all of these things today from healthy men and mentors in your life.

HOW TO WIN AND HOW TO LOSE

Dads and other men teach us how to play games, how to compete fairly and honestly and how to win graciously or lose with dignity. I am deeply appreciative of my father for this. When he played a game, he played as hard as he could. But he always played fairly and had fun doing it, and I always had a sense that as hard as I tried to win, the most important thing truly was how I played the game. And that included whether or not I had fun.

TO BEGIN AND END/RISK WITH WISDOM

Some of us are pretty good at getting things started but we have a heck of a time finishing them. Others do fine once we get started, but we have a hard time beginning. This has to do with *initiating* and *completion*. Initiation is always a risk because we are responsible for what happens after that.

Making something happen in our lives is scary, and a dad or father figure can help us to get going and move forward with our lives. Completion is also scary, because when we are done, it's done. *Then* it can be evaluated. If I never quite finish this book, it will never get published and then you will never have a chance to say if you like it or not. Dads can teach us to stick our necks out. If they support us after we stick our necks out and help us learn from our mistakes, then we won't get stuck in life very often. If they support and demand our completion of something, then we will start to experience the joys and rewards of accomplishment. If they know when to risk and when to stay safe, then we will learn wisdom as well.

TO BE WITH MEN

Many of us who grew up in unhealthy families find it easy to be with women. This often has to do with lack of fathering and also enmeshment with our mothers. We say things like, "All men are just mindless insensitive jerks. I'd rather spend time with sensitive intuitive women." As we heal our childhood wounds, we discover that many men are safe to be with, and that even some "stereotypical men" also have something of value to offer the world. As we become more comfortable with our masculinity, we become more and more able to negotiate the rules and expectations of the male world.

As you begin to learn about yourself as a man, you will notice that men have certain ways of communicating that are different than women's. Men have some unique ways of honoring one another, for example.

That's why films like *Avalon*, *Field Of Dreams* and *Dances With Wolves* are important for us to see and so emotionally powerful. Go back and see those films again with an eye toward how the men interrelate with each other. They are truly masterpieces in this regard. Notice how the son, the father and the grandfather relate to each other in *Avalon*.

In *Field Of Dreams*, let yourself feel all that you feel as Archie Graham turns back into "Doc" Graham, and then is honored for his decision by the other ball players. Look at the eye contact between Ray Kinsella and John Kinsella, or how the camera focuses on the muscles in their arms as they shake hands. Notice the role of good-natured teasing, of healthy competition.

Dances With Wolves is filled with examples of men honoring and supporting each other, especially non-verbally — from the fierce challenging by Wind In His Hair and the thoughtful curiosity and respect of Kicking Bird to the negotiating for possessions, the decision-making processes and respect for individual and group decisions, and the powerfully respectful goodbyes. Notice the facial expressions, the postures, the glances and the smiles. Men communicate a lot with each other. We just need a man to teach us how, by his example.

TO BE WITH WOMEN

Our fathers or other men in our lives can teach us how to be with women in healthy ways, too. Men who did not get healthy fathering do not interact with women in good ways. We get seductive with women in a Don Juan kind of way or in helpless little boy kinds of ways. We have that female dependency I wrote about earlier. Or we abuse women in more overt ways. We may hate women or fear them. We attribute magical powers to women instead of seeing them as complementary to us.

In other words, we either put women on pedestals, in the gutter or both. Without adequate fathering from men, we let women use and abuse us. We give our power away to women. Then we rage at them outwardly or we rage at them inwardly by being passive-aggressive. We get into what I call "gamey" relationships with women where there is no love, just an ongoing contest. The contest becomes: "Let's see who can get their needs met the most, get hurt the least and give as little as possible." These kinds of relationships with women are very destructive.

If we were lucky, we saw the men around us being respectful with women but also respectful of themselves. We saw our dad and mom negotiate cleanly and clearly. When they fought, it was healthy. We had a sense that they liked each other, that they were good companions as well as lovers. We saw them respect each other's vulnerability as well as each other's unique power within the relationship. As a result, we grew up to *like* women rather than trying to be like women. Instead of treating women like objects of sexual release, we learned to treat women as people. Instead of fearing women, hating women or being addicted to women, we learned to enjoy women as 50% of the human race. A good, strong man can teach us about these things.

TO LEARN HOW TO LEARN FROM MEN

This does *not* mean that Dad has to like only stereotypical "guy" things, by any means. For that matter, a lot of guy things are also "girl things" nowadays, anyway. Many women change the oil in their cars, check their batteries, mow the lawn, shovel snow, fix leaky pipes and enjoy football, too.

More than anything, we need to learn some things from our dads. Maybe your dad doesn't repair things around the house, but he's good at accounting or law. Maybe he's a plumber and can teach you that, but he doesn't know much about wiring the house. I know this may sound vague, but think about it. If my dad takes the time to teach me something, then I have received fathering from him, even if it's something that a mom could have taught me. If Dad teaches me, I have had the marvelous experience of having a man nurture me, guide me and teach me. If Dad abuses me while he teaches me, by shaming, criticizing and getting angry, then I have had an awful experience. No wonder so many Adult Children of abusive families have problems with bosses, mentors and other authority figures. We never learned how to learn from men in these families.

Sometimes men are more abrupt or even gruff in their teaching styles, but even this can be okay as long as there is nurturing and respect of the child beneath the gruffness. In fact, this can even be an advantage for boys in some cases.

TO BE A TEAM PLAYER

Because of organized team sports such as football and soccer, men learn something that women do not. Being a "team player" is a very valuable skill, especially in a complex society. Learning rules of "fair play," learning how to win and lose and learning how to give your all but defer to the group when necessary are essential for our survival. A healthy father can teach a boy how to compete fairly, when to be individualistic and when to work for the good of the group or team. A good balance between separateness and group spirit is what we should be shooting for here.

TO SURRENDER/BE SPIRITUAL/PRAY

The most powerful men I know are very humble and not at all "wimpy." If you find this confusing, don't get discouraged. It took me 35 years to figure it out. I had to be brought to my knees by my alcoholism to understand the difference between grandiosity and true power. Because of that, I am grateful for my alcoholism. Powerful people know when to surrender and when to fight. A victim is always surrendering or always fighting but never finds balance. In our surrender, we admit our humanity and in dealing with it, we become more spiritual, holy and powerful. In *Catching Fire*, Merle Fossum does a beautiful job of discussing the role of surrender and spirituality in men's recovery. I encourage you to read what he has to say.

A powerful father who knows the importance of surrender will teach his children how to be powerful, even in the face of old age. As Robert Peck points out, he will face his declining physical prowess with dignity and grace rather than with rage and denial. As Dad grows older, he will acquire more and more wisdom, which will make up for his loss of physical strength.

As he approaches his own death, a powerful father will make peace with his past and surrender to his death without being a victim of it, thereby freeing his children to live the rest of their lives in joy and anticipation rather than in fear and trepidation.

A powerful father knows the meaning of the phrase, "He won the battle but lost the war." He knows that we all lose some of life's battles, that the real skill is in knowing which ones to fight and which ones to release.

A strong father knows how to pray in the broad sense of the word. He knows how to humble himself before God, nature, the universe or whatever he defines as his Higher Power. By humbling himself, he lets his children know that there is more out there than just us and that we need not fear the unknowable. Prayer also allows us to have the excitement, awe and wonder about the universe that keeps each of us young, no matter how old our bodies become.

TO GUIDE, TEACH AND LEAD

We have all experienced those rare teachers who seem to have a special knack for teaching. Many of us have been fortunate enough to experience bosses or managers who get the best performance out of us in a way that leaves us admiring them instead of hating them. Some of us had coaches who honed our skills while keeping us motivated and feeling good about ourselves. Truly effective leadership skills are worth more than gold.

A leader is someone who takes us somewhere new. He gets us to go beyond ourselves. He takes us into uncharted territory. He sees something in us that we cannot see, then he helps us to find and develop it. A good leader does all this and leaves us feeling better than when we began.

In my work with physicians and psychologists, both as individual clients and on a consulting basis, it saddens me to see how many have been wounded by the medical school or graduate school experience. These men are technically trained and skilled but are so damaged by their training they are in danger of losing either their careers, their families, themselves or all of the above. In recent years I have been approached by medical and graduate school faculty who are at last becoming concerned enough to want to change this abuse. It won't happen soon enough for me.

Fathers are the first men in our lives who have the opportunity to lead us. How we feel about the way we are led will have long-lasting effects on how we respond to being led as adults. Even more so, the way our fathers lead us will determine in large part how we try to lead others. Good leaders are always challenging themselves to move forward in their own development, which is good, because it leaves room for us to move forward in *our* development. A small, frightened, inadequate leader is afraid of those he leads. He is threatened by them. So he treats them abusively. He keeps them frustrated and he sabotages their growth and development. He despises the competition from younger men rather than wanting it.

I like my life now. I like the fact that I am getting older. This is without doubt the best stage of my life so far and I look forward with relish and excitement to the next stage. But it wasn't always that way. I used to be petty, fearful, rigid and threatened by others. I like it a lot more the way it is now.

TO LIKE OUR BODIES

This always seems to make men squirm. We don't quite know what to do about our bodies. Back in the 1970s, women intellectuals wrote about the dehumanizing experiences that boys had to endure in high school locker rooms.

Many of us grew up feeling that we had to apologize for having a penis and testicles, beards and body hair. Sometimes this was because of our mothers. But let's face it. If we learned it from our mothers, what were our dads doing to change it? It doesn't take an astrophysicist to figure out that if Mom hated our male bodies, she must have hated Dad's male body, too. And if Dad's male body was being hated and he didn't do anything to stop the hatred, then he probably hated his body and felt the need to apologize for it, too.

A father who is comfortable with his body will have a realistic body image. He will care about his body without being obsessed with it, and he won't feel apologetic about being male. Women seem to like men who are comfortable with themselves. Not arrogant. Not ashamed, but just plain comfortable. We can learn this from Dad.

TO HAVE OUR FEELINGS APPROPRIATELY

What? How to have our feelings appropriately? Yes, I think so. The cognitive-developmental theory of sex-typing proposed by Lawrence Kohlberg of Harvard University suggests that little boys actively seek out men in order to learn how to be male. Little girls do the same with women. It makes sense to me. At a very early age, we notice that there is indeed a difference between males and females. Once we have established this fact, we seek out men, and like little sponges, we soak up all that we see men doing. We do all we can to become like them.

When a man comes to me and says that he wants to do "feelings work," I always say that you don't learn to feel, you learn to not feel. I tell him the story of a little boy whose favorite grandfather died. At the funeral the little boy stood with his head arched back as he looked up into the faces of all his elders. He felt very sad, but he wanted to behave "appropriately," so he tried to take his cues from the adults, especially the men. But all the adults had come from a very inhibited family system and ethnic background: they didn't express feelings very openly. The little boy felt huge tears welling up in his eyes but as he looked at the frozen stoic faces of all the adults in the room, his tears disappeared behind a Cloak-Of-Family-Feeling-Shame.

It was a very sad moment in the little boy's life because his grandfather's funeral could have been his first opportunity to deal with loss in a healthy way. Instead it became the day his feelings began to Go Underground. I state it that way because the only way for our feelings to die is for us to die. Simply by the power of his example, a healthy and strong father will teach his sons about feelings by having his own feelings in healthy ways. When he is deeply sad, he will cry. When he is angry, he will get mad without raging or pouting. When he is scared, he'll say, "I'm scared." When he is lonely, he'll say that he is lonely.

Most important of all, a healthy dad will not just verbalize his feelings, but he will feel his feelings, which can be a very different thing.

Psychologists estimate that 80% of our emotional messages are sent by our nonverbal language, which makes our words much less important than our facial expression, tone of voice, body posture and so on. We learn so much from Dad without even knowing it.

TO BE POLITICAL

Especially if you grew up in an alcoholic or dysfunctional family, the whole idea of politics will probably make your hair stand on end.

"I'm not a political kind of person, and I think that all politics stink!" Ever heard that or said that before? There's only one problem with it. A world without politics can't exist. Any time you get more than one person in a room for more than five minutes, you have politics.

In some of our Lifeworks Clinics, participants have roommates. You've encountered this situation yourself, I'm sure. The two of you get into the room, politely (notice the root word) claim your spaces, exchange pleasantries and prepare for the workshop. As you both begin to exit the room, your roommate rushes back quickly and throws open the window as he exclaims, "I have to have the room cold when we get back. I can't sleep in a warm room." Bingo! The politics just began.

Politics is about living in the world with other human beings and getting your needs met with a minimum of harm to yourself and others. It is about negotiation, compromise and good old debate. It involves the use of personal power and influence. Hopefully your brand of politics also includes respect for the rights and dignity of your fellow humans. But to say that you don't believe in politics is to admit that you are emotionally stuck back in early childhood. It just doesn't work to try to get through life without politics, unless you plan to be socially isolated the rest of your life.

A good dad can help you learn to get your needs met in a spirit of cooperation without becoming a victim. You learn by watching him in his everyday life. You watch how he handles conflicts with your mom, friends, business associates and others. You learn by negotiating your own needs with him. If he lets you win some of the negotiations because you have stated your case well, rather than always having to win, then you will be affirmed in taking those kinds of risks with others, in other situations.

TO BE COMMITTED

Men are notorious for having problems with commitment, which makes me wonder how we have lasted this long, to tell you the truth. Commitment is such a focal part of life. Men are most often accused of not being able to commit to relationships but I see many men having great difficulty with commitment of themselves to a set of beliefs and values or to a career. You might not see it right away, but it is a big risk to commit to something. The fear of what might happen if I commit is one thing that stops me. Another is that I haven't risked trying out different lifestyles and relationships so I don't know enough about myself to know what to commit to.

Dads who have taken the big risks to discover themselves and then have firmly committed themselves to an identity, values and lifestyle, clearly make it easier for their children to do the same. Dads who always "hang so loose" that they can never be "pinned down" produce children who don't trust themselves or others and are not themselves trustworthy.

Commitment is seemingly so simple, too. Much of it is just about follow-through. I say I'll meet you for dinner at 7:00 p.m. on Friday, and lo and behold, I show up for dinner Friday evening, not Saturday evening. I say that I love you in an exclusive sense, and then as a result, I don't have an affair with someone else. I promise not to invade your country with my army, and then I don't invade your country. I profess to be in recovery from an addiction, and, therefore, do what I need to do to stay sober, such as going to AA, getting back into therapy when I fear I might relapse and so on.

Yes, a man can be too responsible and committed. The extremes are usually dysfunctional. There must be room in life for risk, change and flexibility. Play and fun are as important to our lives and health as are food and water. And a healthy dad can teach us by his example to balance play and commitment. He will not rip us off by letting us down all the time after making a promise to us, nor will he rip us off by being an example of a playful, fun-loving offender who believes that the world revolves around him. He will help us find true balance in our lives, not just pseudo-balance. The balance will be real and inside us, not just on the outside for show.

DADS ARE GOOD FOR A LOT

When I brainstorm ideas for a chapter such as this, I usually have scores of little pieces of paper on which I have written my thoughts. Sometimes it's a nugget of wisdom that comes to me while I am commuting to my satellite office across town. At other times, it is an entire list of ideas under one topic heading. Perhaps the best way to end this chapter is to duplicate here some of the things that were on my list entitled:

What Are Dads Good For/What Do We Need From Them?

- To love
- To like us
- To be proud of us
- To spend time with us
- To have "a catch" with us
- To expect us to grow up
- To help separate us from Mom when we get older
- To hug us without being "wimpy" or "macho"
- To teach us "guy things"
- To model respect of self
- To model respect of others
- To stand up for our beliefs
- To stand up for themselves
- To be a team-player
- To take a difficult stand alone
- To be political
- To "make it" in the world
- To be determined
- To care
- To lead, guide and teach
- To surrender
- To pray
- To have faith
- To hope
- To lead us out into the world
- To help us to have wisdom
- To like our bodies

- To risk intelligently and wisely
- To find our power
- To use our power respectfully
- To have integrity and honor
- To be able to commit
- To play without always having to win
- To win
- To lose
- To work
- To be with men
- To be with women
- To feel
- To laugh
- To think
- To begin
- To follow-through
- To end

There are many more specific things that we can learn from Dad or that we need from Dad. I encourage you to add to this list as you see fit. And please don't trap yourself into a life of misery by saying that you didn't get what you needed from your father when you were little so you are doomed forever. Remember . . .

You can get the fathering you need from any healthy man who is able and willing to give it. In some cases, you can even get it from someone who is younger than you.

3

AND GOD MADE THEM MALE AND FEMALE

The two sexes mutually corrupt and improve each other.

Mary Wollstonecraft
A Vindication of the Rights of Women

7

Who's Better: Men Or Women?

hy can't a woman be more like a man, and a man more like a woman? Well, the answer is that they can be, and they can't be. Confused? We've been confusing each other for thousands of years.

In truth, women and men have been getting more like each other than ever before, at least in industrialized, high-tech societies, because the need for specialization of survival tasks has diminished. A woman can drive a high-tech tank in battle just as well as a man. Physical strength differences aren't nearly as important as they once were.

Because many men don't have to be out "hunting and gathering" miles from home for days at a time, they can be just as involved or even more involved in daily child care than women. Women have proven that they can lead successful businesses, although very few have made it into the top spots in major corporations, a fact due to the "good ol' boy" network more than anything else, I suspect. There are a lot of women doctors and lawyers, where once there were few. There are a lot of men who are overcoming their shame about tears, too.

So where is it all leading us? Will we end up someday with men and women being identical except that men have penises and testicles and women have vaginas and uteruses and ovaries? We have the cute little image that's reproduced in artwork and greeting cards, showing the little boy looking into his diaper and the little girl looking into her diaper, and they both exclaim, "There is a difference!" But is that all there is? *Are* genitals the only difference?

SEX DIFFERENCES

There are scores of studies in the literature that demonstrate enduring physical, emotional and behavioral differences between males and females. Some of these are due to hormones, such as testosterone and androgens, while others are purported to be due to structural differences in the brain, the skeletal system or muscles.

I remember an ingenious study done by Jerome Kagan of Harvard University in which he generated random shapes, some of which were rounded and "soft" while others were more angular and "hard." He showed these shapes to children from a number of different cultures, including some very primitive ones. After the children looked at them, Kagan asked them to tell him which ones were "male" and which ones were "female." The resounding consensus among the children were that the angular, hard shapes were male. As much as we would like to believe otherwise, there are some pretty deep, unconscious perceptions that we all carry about men and women.

In the early days of the women's movement, I was especially impressed with a book that is now considered to be *the* classic in the field, *The Psychology of Sex Differences*. Psychologists Eleanor Maccoby of Stanford University and

Carol Jacklin, now at USC, integrated, analyzed and interpreted most of the research and data on sex differences up to that date. College students back then were fascinated by the findings, many of which still hold true today.

Women love to hear they are "biologically superior" to men in certain ways right from the start. At conception, women have two X chromosomes at the 23rd-pair location (XX), while men have an XY there. The "Y" is just a fragment of a chromosome. Therefore, it causes all kinds of problems in males. Or so the theory goes. It is believed that more spontaneous abortions and stillbirths are male, that more males have birth defects and that more males are hyperactive (minimal brain dysfunction/attention deficit disorder). They have more learning disabilities, have behavior problems in school, are more demanding during infancy and die more frequently during infancy.

The research on hormonal differences between men and women is fascinating, too. If you take male rats and put them in a cage with an activity wheel and then measure their activity, aggressiveness and so on, their activity levels and levels of aggressiveness are significantly higher than female rats' levels. If you then inject female rats with testosterone, they suddenly start acting a lot more like the males.

In humans if a female fetus is exposed to increased levels of testosterone while in the mother's womb, what often happens is that the baby will be born with normal female genitals, but also with rudimentary male genitals. This extra tissue which might have been a penis and scrotum is surgically removed at birth so that the little girl is then physically normal in every way. But what psychologists have discovered later on is that these little girls behave in certain ways like little boys. How? When they are seven and eight years old, they seem to be more physically active and aggressive, play rough more often and fight a little more. As Carol Jacklin pointed out in 1989, research on the effects of hormones on boys and girls is not as clear as the earlier animal studies would suggest. In summarizing several studies, she noted that fluctuations in hormone levels affected behavior the most, that boys and girls were affected differently by the same hormones.

In 1974 Maccoby and Jacklin concluded that in general, girls were superior to boys in verbal skills. Boys were better at spatial relationships (map-reading, rotating objects in three-dimensional space, etc.) and math, and were more aggressive. In Jacklin's 1989 review article in the *American Psychologist*, she noted that boys and girls have become more similar in verbal and other intellectual abilities over the past decade. The only exception she noted was that there are still more boys at the very high end of the math ability continuum.

WHAT DOES IT ALL MEAN?

There are many more documented and disputed differences between males and females, and I'm sure that the research and controversy will continue. Men and women will always be curious about what makes the other tick. Before we move on, it is important to remember the following:

1. Many of the biological differences between men and women are not very strong. This means that men as a group may be more physically aggressive than women, but that a specific woman may be more aggressive than a specific man.

2. Learning and cultural influences can often over-ride the biological differences. For example, there are some true biological reasons why men as a group do not cry as readily as women beyond the obvious cultural shame that American men have about crying.

   Dr. William Frey who founded the Tear Research Center at St. Paul-Ramsey Medical Center has found that boys and girls prior to puberty cry about the same, but after puberty, they don't. Prolactin in women's bloodstreams permits them to cry more readily than men, too. But a specific man may actually cry much more than a specific woman because of environment. We see this a lot with men who unconsciously carry the sadness, pain and shame of their family systems so that they are constantly overwhelmed by their own and others' problems. These men do the opposite of the typical "shut-down male" — they cry all the time, which is just as dysfunctional as not crying enough.

3. The next thing to remember is that men and women *are* different, but that the ways in which we express those differences are very important. To say that sexism has been a part of life for thousands of years is an understatement. In ancient Greece and Rome, it was an accepted practice to kill all but one female infant because they weren't valued as much as males. Women have been raped, battered and abused throughout history because men have always had the superiority of physical strength at their advantage. Men's physical aggressiveness, our testosterone level so to speak, has been used to explain the constant wars and atrocities that have occurred throughout history as well.

I believe that there is some truth to this thesis, as popularized by Susan Brownmiller in *Against Our Will: Men, Women And Rape.* Hormones do not give men a license to rape or kill. But I should also add that hormones do not give women a license to ragefully abuse men, children and other women. There have been many powerful and destructive women throughout history, too.

You may be shocked to learn that in a major study cited by Warren Farrell in 1986, the amount of physical spouse abuse of women by men was matched by that of men by women. I believe it is time for male and female people to start treating each other with mutual power and respect.

4. We have choices as to how we express ourselves. We have choices as to how we use our biological strengths and limits. I can choose to drink alcohol because I have inherited the genes of alcoholism or I can admit my disease and surrender to treatment for it. I can treat my hypertension with medication, diet and exercise, or I can choose to leave it untreated and die of a stroke or heart disease later on. A woman with PMS can get support and help for it or she can say that she has PMS and use it as an excuse to hurt those she loves. And a man can say that he has a strong

sex drive or a need to conquer and fight because of testosterone and use that as an excuse to rape or kill. Or he can choose to be humane, civilized and healthy by channeling his biology into something productive. In other words *all* of us, men and women alike, need to be accountable for who we are and what we do. Blaming sex differences for our abuse of each other doesn't cut it anymore.

5. The last thing to remember about sex differences is that the learned differences are very strong as noted above. These strong learned, cultural differences between men and women are often referred to as sex-role stereotypes, and they have done a lot to make men and women miserable.

THE MODEL OF PSYCHOLOGICAL ANDROGYNY

We have been studying, researching and writing legislation about sex-role stereotypes for the past 25 years, and in many ways we're still as confused as ever. I believe part of our confusion stems from the fact that stereotypes seem to have a kernel of truth to them. They don't just materialize from thin air. On the other hand, the problems with them is that:

1. Stereotypes are based on distortions and/or prejudices that are misleading and damaging.
2. Stereotypes are rigid and leave no room for individual needs, wants, values or talents.
3. They encourage us to judge each other in extreme terms.

As a group, men seem to be less able to cry than women, and this appears to have some basis in biological fact. Does this mean that all men are "unfeeling bastards"? Does this mean that all women are more sensitive than men? Based on your stereotype of men, can you be sure that Jim Smith is an unemotional brute who only thinks about breasts, beer and the bottom line? The chances are higher that Jim Smith is a little more analytical and a little less feeling than his woman friend — but an unfeeling brute? Maybe, maybe not. I would encourage you to talk to him first before making such a drastic critical judgment.

In the early '70s, psychologist Sandra Bem began her pioneering work on sex-role stereotyping and the concept of psychological androgyny, employing the Bem Sex-Role Inventory which she designed. The BSRI has 20 items that are stereotypically "male," 20 items that are stereotypically "female," and 20 items that she deemed to be neutral. Using this inventory, Bem was able to categorize men and women as masculine, feminine, androgynous and so on. She and her colleagues then conducted a series of ingenious experiments to see if indeed the androgynous men and women were better off than others.

What Bem discovered was that in general, androgynous men and women were better able to handle the widest range of real-life situations, such as being independent or playing with an infant. In other words, stereotypical masculine men were good at doing "guy stuff" but not much else. Stereotypical women were the worst off, doing well only when offered the task of listening passively to another person's problems. From these and other studies, Bem and her colleagues concluded that the healthiest woman has both male and female personality traits available to her, and the healthiest man has both male and female traits available to him, when the situation requires it.

STEREOTYPIC MEN AND WOMEN, HEALTHY MEN AND WOMEN

Marilyn Frost, Graduate Dean at St. Mary's College Graduate Institute in Minneapolis, devised a briefer and modified version of the BSRI to be used in classroom lectures back in the '70s. I have modified that version even further over the years. Because I feel that this material on androgyny is so important in our understanding of men and women today, I want to show you how it works. I will first present the picture of the stereotypic woman and the stereotypic man, with a discussion of how the extremes are the real dysfunction; then I will present a composite picture of a healthy adult based on the healthy portions of those stereotypes.

To begin, please refer to the left side of Table 7.1 in which I present *some* of the traits typically attributed to females in our culture.

Table 7.1. Stereotypic Women

Traditional Female Traits	Maladaptive Form
Dependent	Helpless
Passive	Victim
Gentle	Weak
Home-centered	Stagnant
Tactful, ethical	Self-denying
Feeling	Emotional wallowing

FRIEL 1978

As you peruse this list, think about these traits. Are they healthy? Unhealthy? Not sure? Frankly, they are all healthy! If we weren't dependent, we'd be in big trouble. Each of us depends on thousands of other human beings every day. There are times when it is very important to be passive, for instance, when we have no control over a situation such as a flight delayed due to weather. A great way to shorten our lives is to get as angry and steamed-up as we can about the frustrations in life over which we have no control. Being gentle surely can't be all bad, nor can being home-centered. After all, if somebody weren't gentle and home-centered we would all be violent and there wouldn't be any homes to live in.

We would be in big trouble if no one were ever ethical and tactful, and the world would be awfully cold and heartless if there were no humans who emphasized feelings rather than analysis. Do you see it? Not one of these traits is negative. So what's the big deal, you ask? Where's the problem?

In working with survivors of dysfunctional families, Linda and I have found that it is the extremes of these traits that define dysfunction. On the right side of Table 7.1, you can see the extremes to the healthy "female" traits I just discussed. Thus our dependency becomes outright helplessness. We get clingy, whiny and needy. We lack maturity and self-reliance.

Our passivity becomes victimization, in which we let others use and abuse us, and in which we believe that we have no power, no choices and no options anymore. Our gentleness becomes weakness, wherein we become overly vulnerable, yielding and "soft." We don't stick up for ourselves or others, and so we often hurt ourselves and others, especially our own children.

The home-centered person becomes stagnant in the extreme, never wanting to try anything new, never wanting to go anywhere new, never wanting to meet anyone new and eventually becoming very bored, very boring or both. The ethical, tactful person becomes self-denying to a troublesome and nauseating degree: "I don't have any needs, I don't have any wants." We become a martyr of the worst kind, not the holy kind. Nobody who is healthy can stand to be around us. And lastly, the extreme side of the feeling person is a person who engages in what I call emotional wallowing, overwhelmed by sadness, pain, hurt, shame, guilt, loneliness, anger or fear which is debilitating to say the least.

Now let's take a similar look at men. As you examine the left side of Table 7.2 notice again that none of the traits listed are unhealthy. They are all healthy traits that define some men. I don't think anyone could argue with the value of independence and being assertive is something to which we all aspire. It's how we declare our likes, dislikes, wants and needs. And how we protect ourselves. I also believe that being competitive is a very important part of life, survival and adaptability; without it we would still be stuck back in caves killing all of our female infants except one per family.

Being adventurous is what keeps us from getting bored and stagnant; taking risks is what allows culture to improve. A person who can be decisive is considered to be healthier than one who can't. After all, if you're always getting stuck and can't decide, you're paralyzed. Constant indecision is surely a sign of emotional dysfunction. And of course, sometimes the decisions we must make are really painful, such as firing someone or ending a hurtful relationship. An active person gets things done, goes places and sees things, and accomplishes much; all of which are important and necessary things for emotional health.

Table 7.2. Stereotypic Men

Traditional Male Traits	Maladaptive Form
Independent	Isolated
Assertive	Hostile, rageful
Competitive	Ruthless
Adventurous	Reckless
Decisive	Unethical, tactless
Active	Emotionally blunted

FRIEL 1978

But what about the dysfunctional side of these male traits? When they get pushed to the extremes, we get the traits shown on the right-hand side of Table 7.2, better known as the "typical male brute." In unhealthy men, our independence turns into social and emotional isolation to the point that we are incapable of having a relationship with fellow human beings, male or female. Our assertiveness turns into hostility and rage, aggressiveness runs amok like the monstrous and tormented Mr. Hyde.

Our healthy competitive urges turn into damaging ruthlessness, in which we don't care at all for others' dignity, lives or our own environment. Our own survival becomes so important that we ignore the rest of humanity and therefore endanger even our own survival, which is the Paradox of Ruthlessness, as I call it.

Our adventurous side turns into recklessness in the extreme, as we expand more and more outside of ourselves to the point of self- and other-destruction. Then our ability to be decisive makes us unethical and tactless, so that we care little for the damaging effects of our decisions. And lastly, when we go to "male extremes," our tendency toward high activity levels makes us emotionally blunted so that we cover up our feelings with more and more "doing."

Look at the right side of Table 7.2. What you see is a highly dysfunctional man who is shut down, angry, empty, lonely, uncaring and terrified without being aware of it. You also have a man who hurts those he "loves," destroys the environment and is incapable of having a relationship with anyone. It isn't a pretty sight.

HEALTHY MEN, HEALTHY WOMEN, HEALTHY PEOPLE

The big question now is, "So what?" What does all of this mean? We have a list of healthy and unhealthy female traits and a list of healthy and unhealthy male traits. Now what? First, remember that these lists are only partial, but for the sake of simplicity, let's just use the ones I've listed. What the research suggests is that a healthy person, whether a man or a woman, has access to *all* of these traits in differing amounts, as shown in Table 7.3. This means that regardless of gender, a healthy man *or* woman can be independent and dependent, assertive and passive, competitive and gentle, adventurous and home-centered, decisive and ethical, as well as active and feeling-oriented. That's pretty simple, neat and tidy, isn't it?

Or is it? Aren't we right back to saying that men and women should ultimately be *exactly* the same except for physical differences? I am going to go out on a limb here and say, "No," and then take some of it back by saying, "Sometimes." I believe that there will always be some clear, though very subtle psychological/emotional differences between men and women no matter how liberated we become and that the sooner we admit that, the better off we'll all be. If you want to call me a dinosaur for saying that, okay. The worst that will happen to me is that my thinking will become extinct when at last this idea is proven wrong. Until then, I'm sticking with my premise.

Table 7.3. Healthy Men And Women

Healthy Adult Traits	
Independent	Dependent
Assertive	Passive
Competitive	Gentle
Adventurous	Home-centered
Decisive	Tactful, ethical
Active	Feeling

FRIEL 1978

I believe that there is something called "maleness" and something called "femaleness," and that there is something called "personness," for lack of a better word. I believe that in our heart-of-hearts, deep inside of us, we men have unconscious urges to be logical, to explore, to play in the mud, to control everything with technology, to build, to expand and to protect our territory. I am not saying that women do not also have these urges. But I think that in a very primitive part of our psyches we *do* have these urges more than women have them.

I also believe that in that same place, women have a very deep unconscious urge to create a safe, unspoiled home environment, to care for family and the group, to nurture and feel the pulse of creation, to guard the spirit and feelings of humanity. I am not saying that men do not also have these urges. But listen to feminists, if you will. Listen to philosophers and theologians. Listen to enlightened social thinkers. Listen to the 10 o'clock news. As the environment gets closer and closer to irreparable damage, as we stand on the brink of yet another war, as we fall further into the depths of addiction in our culture, what is everyone saying? They are saying, "We need women in power. We need feminine leadership. We need someone who will put our homes (the environment) ahead of conquering, building and destroying. We need someone who will be more ethical and caring." What all of these people are loudly implying is that there is a difference between men and women!

In Figure 7.1 I have drawn what I believe represents the relationship between maleness, femaleness and personness. I believe that as men learn from women and as women learn from men, the part described as *personness* will overlap more; but that there will always be a part of both circles that is reserved just for men, and one that is reserved just for women. Without those separate parts, there would be no dynamic tension in the universe, no social or cultural evolution and life would be pretty darned boring.

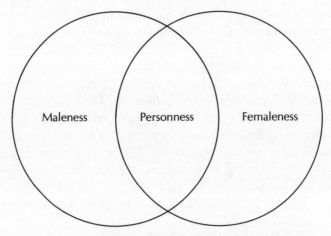

Figure 7.1. The relationship between our maleness, our femaleness and our "personness."

8

Males And Females Together

BOYS AND GIRLS AND OTHER PUZZLES

or many years Linda and I have chosen to conduct separate men's and women's therapy groups for the majority of our clients who are in ongoing groups, with the understanding that mixed therapy groups can be very important and even necessary for one's healing. In our Lifeworks Clinic, which is a four-day healing program for family-of-origin and Adult Child, co-dependency issues, we do mix men and women because it is close-ended and quite structured. Our reasons for separating men and women in ongoing group are three-fold:

1. One of the key symptoms of coming out of an unhealthy family is that we have trouble relating

95

to our own gender. Men say it is easier to be close to women, and women say it is easier to be close to men. As a result, we lack a sense of safety with members of our own sex, and we lack respect for ourselves as men and women.

2. Before clients have clear boundaries around intimacy and sexuality, they tend to confuse the two. This makes it difficult and less efficient to get through the core intimacy work. There can be a lot of group energy expended on dealing with romantic or sexual feelings, which is fine later on, but basically a hindrance in the early stages of recovery.

3. In natural settings, boys and girls segregate themselves for most of childhood, which appears to be both normal and healthy. Something is learned in this unique bonding with our own gender, and if that process is interrupted or otherwise corrupted, it makes it impossible for men and women to complete their early adulthood identity crisis work. The research on social interaction between boys and girls sheds some fascinating light on this last dynamic.

In her excellent research review article in the April 1990 *American Psychologist*, Eleanor Maccoby looks at over 50 studies that confirm what many of us already knew, but with some twists that may also surprise you. Boys and girls averaging under three years of age clearly demonstrated more social behavior when with same sex peers than when with opposite sex peers. The oft-assumed passivity of girls isn't so clear-cut either. In the same study, they found that little girls were no more passive than little boys. But they were much more passive when paired with a little boy than when paired with another little girl.

In support of what we have known clinically for years, Maccoby and Jacklin found solid evidence for children's preference for same-sex playmates even at early ages. At age 4½, children spend up to three times more time with kids of the same sex. By age 6½ they were spending up to 11 times more time playing with others of the same sex. In summarizing a lot of literature in this area, Maccoby stated, "Gender segregation is a widespread phenomenon. It is found in all the cultural settings in which children are in social groups large enough to permit choice." In other words, boys would rather play with boys, and girls would rather play with girls. This seems to hold true under a wide range of conditions, and it is important to note that adult pressure for boys and girls to play together is one of the few things that changes this behavior (Eisenhart & Holland, 1983; Thorne 1986), and it only works while the pressure is being applied, in my experience.

The studies reviewed by Maccoby are even more interesting, because they shed some light on why boys and girls/men and women behave with and toward each other the way they do. Essentially, these studies suggest that boys are much more involved in competition, dominance and rough play than are girls. In their attempts at influencing others, girls tend to influence much more by polite suggestions rather than force or domination. Furthermore, boys are more likely to ignore girls' attempts to influence them, but girls do not ignore boys' attempts. In fact, girls seem to find boys' influence styles unappealing and choose to play with other girls, rather than be dominated by boys, which makes sense to me.

Boys also prefer to play with other boys rather than with girls, and they prefer to play outside more (Kraft & Vraa, 1975). They tend to form friendships around mutual interests (Erwin, 1985) rather than sharing personal confidences. When girls' relationships break up, they feel more pain and stress than boys feel when their friendships break up.

In looking at verbal communication styles, Maccoby cites the classic review by Maltz and Borker, who list the now familiar differences between boys in all-boy groups and girls in all-girl groups. Put simply, boys are more aggressive and commanding when they "hang out" together. They threaten, brag, command, direct, joke, try to outdo each other and interrupt more than girls do in all-girl groups. As Maccoby put it so well, for boys, "speech serves largely egoistic functions and is used to establish and protect an individual's turf. Among girls, conversation is a more socially binding process."

In noting all of these differences, in which we get a picture of boys being pretty tough and individualistic and girls being pretty cooperative and group-oriented, Maccoby makes it clear that boys' and mens' styles work for them, just as girls' styles work for them.

What begins to emerge from all of this research is that boys and girls, men and women, have some pretty strong tendencies to communicate differently and that neither of these ways of communicating is bad — they're simply different. But what also emerges is that when you put men and women together, watch out! This is where the "battle of the sexes" turns into all-out war.

Somewhere during adolescence or young adulthood, boys and girls become young men and women. They discover the opposite sex and then start negotiating with each other as partners and lovers. Then all hell breaks loose!

Part of the mysterious, exciting, painful, scary and rewarding process of dating, mating and living in the adult world is the complex process of learning about the opposite sex. Men look at women, scratch their heads and say, "I don't understand women." Women look at men, scratch their heads and say, "I don't understand men." And away we go.

MEN AND WOMEN ASSEMBLING THE PUZZLE

Linda and I believe that what men and women need to understand first is that whether they are gay, straight or bisexual, they need to come to terms with, bond with, identify with and make friends with people of their own sex. Men need to be comfortable with and proud of their maleness. Women need to be comfortable with and proud of their femaleness. We need to learn all of the ins and outs and idiosyncracies of communciating with members of our own sex. We need to learn the rules of men if we are men, and the rules of women if we are women. This is what we're "supposed to be doing" during childhood and adolescence.

Once we have done this herculean task, *then* we are ready to take on the even greater task of learning to negotiate friendships and partnerships with women. It is into this arena that we bring our social differences and our conflicting rules and expectations. It is in this arena that the health or dysfunction of our childhoods is quickly revealed.

How do men and women do it? Women have been struggling with these issues on a planetary scale for centuries. The Women's Movement of the 1960s and 1970s just happened to be the most recent one in America. Women all over the world have been trying to change the rules of communication for a long time. Men have done it in the past by simply overpowering women, the way that little boys overpower little girls in the sandbox at preschool. But as women achieve equality in society, the rules of domination and brute force don't work as well. People don't appreciate those rules as much today. As women gain more and more financial independence from men, they no longer have to put up with the rules of social interaction that they had to accept before. Men and women are thus finding out about each other one step at a time. But what they are doing in the process is rewriting some of the rules. I think this is happening on a global level, just as it happens in every household and boardroom in America.

As women gain some financial independence from men, men need to gain some emotional independence from women. Some men say, "But I need a woman to help me express my feelings. I can only cry if I'm around a woman." This is a dangerous trap that flows from the dangerous emotional rules we learned as boys. The answer is not to learn to cry with women. The answer is not to cry like women. The answer is to cry like a man! Women can't ultimately help us here. They can help along the way, perhaps. But ultimately we will emerge victorious from our traps when we are able to cry, be sad, hurt and share fear and loneliness with men.

As women learn to play by *some* of the good rules by which men play, men also need to learn to play by some of the good rules by which women play. Men need to learn how to affirm others during a conversation, rather than always fighting for turf. We can't keep running around the neighborhood peeing on everything to mark our territory. People will tire of the pee. We need to care about family and community even though we may feel that building, conquering and hunting are our major jobs in life.

Women need to continue to encroach on our territory, so to speak. As women gain more power, men will have to find some of their power in places other than the barrel of a gun. Little girls are very powerful in influencing other little girls by being polite, affirming, cooperating, listening to the other person's side of things and so on. Many men have learned as corporate managers that these are powerful and respectful ways to communicate with others. As we learn from each other, as we struggle to get to know each other and as we do respectful and fair battle with each other, men and women will get better. It happens all the time.

A FAIR-FIGHTING METAPHOR

If you remember back in Chapter 7, I noted that psychological androgyny was a pretty healthy idea whose time has come. I also noted that men would still always be men, and women would still always be women. As little boys and girls grow up and start to date, they do two things:

- Begin to discover the different rules of communication that the other has just spent 21 years learning.
- Begin to try to get their needs met from each other and within their relationship, i.e., they begin to negotiate within and between those two rule systems.

It is at this point that men and women get the opportunity to learn from each other and support each other's growth. As we try to get our needs met in "lover" relationships, we are given the chance to heal many of the wounds that happened to us in our childhoods.

This idea is explained beautifully in Harville Hendrix' 1988 bestseller, *Getting The Love You Want: A Guide For Couples*. According to Hendrix, whatever wounds we still carry from childhood will become part of the equation when we select a mate. In fact, we have long agreed with his belief that we often select a mate who has the negative characteristics of our parents, which unconsciously gives us the chance to heal those old wounds.

Thus if your mother was never emotionally there for you, you may select a mate who is not emotionally there for you. If in your struggles to get your needs met from your partner, you are able to communicate this pain and then your partner is able to become emotionally available to you in new ways, you have then healed an old wound. You've changed the rules. Your partner, who was hurt by learning to be unavailable to others, will heal that part of their wound by becoming available to you. Did you follow all that? If not, read it again. It's very important.

This process is very similar to the one that we work out with individuals doing their family-of-origin/identity work. We try to help our clients first work on this as individuals, and then help them work it through in their partnership. One of the things we notice especially with male-female couples is that some of those communication styles I mentioned earlier in this chapter really need to be worked through. Men and women need to learn each other's languages.

With Linda's permission, I will share an example from our own life together.

When I was growing up, I learned that it was okay to be angry and fight, but I learned it too well. I did what many men do, I used my ability to fight and argue to always get my way. Like a little boy in the sandbox, I simply bulldozed my way through relationships. When Linda was growing up, she learned not to get angry. Her way of living and protecting herself was to withdraw.

You may have noticed that it is very common for one partner to be more overtly powerful and the other to be more covertly powerful. It is this way for us. When we would have a disagreement, or a full-blown fight, I would want to fight and argue it out but that would frighten Linda, and she would want to withdraw.

And so the dance would begin. I would get angry, she would withdraw. As she withdrew, I got scared, but because it wasn't okay for me to express fear, I would get angrier. My fear of abandonment turned into anger, which scared Linda more, and she withdrew more. Can you see the vicious trap we were in? We loved each other dearly but we couldn't bridge the terrible chasm that we kept building with our old wounds. I needed to embrace my fear and vulnerability, and Linda needed to embrace her overt power and anger.

It didn't happen overnight, I can assure you. But over a three to five year period we gradually started to turn that battleship around with a single paddle, until one day in the beginning of a disagreement, Linda let loose with the cleanest healthiest anger I had seen from anybody in a long time. That fight didn't last very long, either. When it was over, we had a new relationship.

I was relieved she had stood her ground with me, and she was relieved that I hadn't abandoned her after she stood toe-to-toe and eye-to-eye with me. I became able to tell her when I was scared or hurt, which was the big piece of work I needed to do here. And she was able to get angry and set boundaries with me, which was her big piece of work here. That period in our marriage marked the beginning of the deepest and safest intimacy I have ever experienced.

As we work with men and women in therapy, Linda and I are touched by the universality of our pain and our struggles. We see couples working so hard to negotiate their gender differences as well as their basic human needs. It is truly awe-inspiring. It has convinced us that lovers *can* live with each other and be fulfilled, and that the healing process does not mean that we must give up our maleness or our femaleness. The healing process means that we must surrender to the unhealthy sides of ourselves so that we can go and develop the healthy sides. Relationships *can* work.

FATHERS AND DAUGHTERS

It is said that a little boy's first love is his mom, and that a little girl's first love is her dad. Freud went so far as to say that we marry our mom or our dad. I believe that much of this is true, with some qualifications. My first experience with females was with my mother and my older sister, so I learned about females from them. Likewise, my daughters' first experiences with men were with me, their father. It is from our opposite-sex parent that we begin to learn some of those intriguing rules of communication that the other sex engages in, too, which is very important.

I have written a lot in this book about fathers and sons, and some about mothers and sons, and many of the same dynamics apply. If a father is distant and aloof with his daughters, they will learn to mistrust men and get involved with men who are not there for them emotionally. If a father uses his daughters as "little moms," for emotional support he should be getting from adult women and men, then they will learn to be comfortable with being used and will grow up to let men use them. If Dad is demanding, controlling and perfectionistic with his daughters, then they will either become demanding of themselves or go to the other extreme as a way of rebelling just like boys do. If Dad sexually abuses his daughters, then they will either become sexually shut down and frightened or sexually promiscuous and addicted. Or they will become attracted to men who are sexually addicted and exploitive.

Perhaps the best way to describe what a healthy father can give to his daughter is to look at what happens when his daughter gets married in our culture. We have a very touching and telling ritual that says it all.

When a little girl is born into the world, she is loved and supported through childhood by a mother and father who love each other with respect and care. Then she enters young adulthood and begins to shift some of her "father bonding" to men outside of her home as she dates, and falls in and out of love. She discovers who she is and what kind of life she wants to have for herself. She grows up more and more each year. Then one day she finds her identity, which includes a tentative career plan, a set of values and beliefs, her sexual preference and a group of people who support her in her adult world, as her family of origin had supported her in her child world.

If her identity includes a long term commitment to a single partner, she finds herself in love with a man (or woman, if that is her preference) with whom she makes a mutual commitment. They plan a wedding ceremony. She walks down the aisle on the arm of the first man she loved — her father. Beaming with pride and joy at his daughter's accomplishment of growing up and creating her own life, her father "gives her away," and in so doing, he says, "You are a woman now. Go out into the world with the knowledge that I will always love you, that you are no longer 'my little girl.' You are a woman." That's how it happens in a healthy family.

When the family has some notable problems as many families do, this process gets sidetracked. In some families it only gets sidetracked a little bit, requiring some mid-course corrections. In other families it get sidetracked a lot and requires major reconstruction. If a little girl is neglected or abused by Mom and Dad, her bonding with boys and men will be disrupted. She may avoid dating altogether until she heals her childhood wounds, or she may get hooked on relationships as a way to try to get the love she didn't get as a child. If she bonded with an abusive dad, she will tend to find men who abuse or neglect her.

If Dad needed his daughter to be there for him instead of the other way around, he will be threatened when she starts to date. Dads like this will accuse their daughters of being "cheap" or promiscuous when they start normal healthy dating. They will grill their daughters after every date, become controlling and act very jealous. They will try to keep their daughters "little" so that they won't "lose" them. Moms do the same thing, too. Or when daughters start to grow up, passive manipulative fathers will get jealous and pout, growing distant and aloof as they try to punish their daughters for "cheating on" Dad. These dads will act like jealous lovers instead of proud fathers. This dynamic is very sad and destructive.

WHAT DO DAUGHTERS WANT FROM THEIR FATHERS?

I spoke with a number of women about their fathers — what they got, what they didn't get and what they wished they had got. It was a powerful experience for me, the father of two daughters.

The clearest and simplest explanation I heard came from Lynda Winter, Director of our Lifeworks Clinic in Dayton, Ohio. She works a powerful program of recovery and has "walked the walk" as we say in recovery circles. She said that she got all the time and attention from her dad that she needed until she was about four years old, then her dad "left" emotionally but not physically, leaving her with a deep father wound. She said that in the last few years of his life she finally got what she needed from him. As I listened intently to her story, I sat breathlessly on the edge of my chair, waiting to hear the complex description of what she finally got from him.

What came next was very profound, but it wasn't complicated. Lynda said that what she needed from her father was *to know who he was as a man.* There was a long silence as I let the words sink in. She said that in the last few years of his life, her father revealed who he was — he was shy, he had shame and he had emotional vulnerability. She needed him "not to just be a provider, but to be there emotionally. To learn his history. To learn what it was like for him to grow up. To be a role-model for what a good husband is like. To respect women." The last thing she said was that women need to be cared for by men, but not to be taken care of, because when men and women "take care of" each other, they end up *taking rather than giving*. I think Lynda said it all.

We who are fathers of daughters need to grow up ourselves so that our needs are being met by other adults. We need to find our feelings and start having them. We need to share them in ways that are appropriate for the age of our daughters. We shouldn't get enmeshed with our daughters by sharing feelings that are overwhelming to them. But neither do we need to hide who we are. As we do with our sons' manhood, we need to celebrate our daughters' womanhood. We need to support their growing up.

We need to be a part of their lives and be there when they need us, and then we need to let go of them as they launch themselves out into the world. We need to help the launching process by letting them know that our wives or partners are the most important relationships in our lives. We will always love our daughters, but their job in growing up is to go out of the home and create their own lives and love relationships. There needs to be a firm but gentle boundary. We need to celebrate when they bond with other adults, both men and women. We need to watch in the wings with excitement and anticipation as they struggle to grow. When they're little, we let them fall down and skin their knees learning to walk, and we need to let them "fall down and skin their knees" as they leave home and try to find work, love and a meaningful lifestyle.

Dads, if you believe that you haven't "done it right," please remember that it is never too late to correct mistakes. Mistakes are human. Wounds can be healed. Lynda Winter's dad did it in the last few years of his life. You can start right now. Let the healing begin.

MOTHERS AND SONS

My Mother

My mother was the daughter of an alcoholic father. From all that I can tell, her mother worked herself ragged trying to keep the family together. As the third child, my mother seemed to be equally enmeshed and protective of both her parents. She finally admitted her father's alcoholism to me just a few short months before she died. Like my father, she was a painful contrast between a woman who was intelligent, warm, loving and joyous on the one hand; and a woman who was scared, ashamed, lonely and angry on the other. Where my father was female dependent, my mother was male dependent. She tried to enlist my brother and me as males to meet the needs my father wasn't able or willing to meet.

For many years I viewed my mother as the victim in the family. I felt sorry for her and tried to rescue and encourage her to do the things with her life she wanted to do but wasn't doing. I became like a parent to her, which meant I was doomed to get into one painful relationship after another when I left home and went out into the world.

As a third child, my "job" as an adult was to shift back and forth from my father's role of the shut-down male, who couldn't be emotionally intimate with a woman, to my mother's script of trying to rescue and "save" women. It was a painful mess for a long time, and I am grateful that I have finally healed enough to have a strong, clear, exciting and caring relationship with Linda.

My mother did many things for which I am also grateful. But like many moms back then, she often did too much for us and not nearly enough for herself. She was a Girl Scout leader and a Cub Scout Leader. She drove us all over creation to lessons and meetings. She and my father went to all of our school events. She was an excellent cook. She had a good sense of humor when she wasn't using it to express her anger or disappointment. She tried to be very spiritual and dabbled all of her life in religious interests. Her faith helped her through years of pain and sorrow but because of her childhood neglect and abuse, she wasn't able to find real peace and serenity until the last year of her life after my father died. The paradox about her religion was that it got her through the pain, but she also used her beliefs as a way to avoid growing up and getting healthy until the very end.

I know that life is difficult at times and I hope that life after death is much better. But I also know that while we're alive, we have thousands of chances to make our lives better and to heal some wounds. To say that "I can't heal" and that "I'll just have to wait to get my reward in heaven" is not what spirituality is about for me but I think that's how my mother saw it.

As my father's alcoholism escalated and her fear and loneliness escalated along with it, she turned to a psychiatrist for help. He helped her become addicted to Valium and sleeping pills. Then she started to smoke and drink to medicate her pain further, becoming multiply chemically dependent.

After several "nervous breakdowns," which were simply total collapses from emotional and physical addiction, she stumbled onto a family physician in San Francisco who knew how to treat "co-dependency" years before the word came into being. He told her to start taking care of herself. He put her in the hospital for rest. He took her off of the drugs she was on. She quit drinking. And her life began to stabilize.

The one piece that was always missing, that no one ever suggested to her, was that both she and my father needed to get into Alcoholics Anonymous. In other words, she quit drinking and trying to take care of her grown children, but she never dealt with the shame and loneliness of addiction and co-dependency by joining a support group of others in the same boat. For that, I still carry sadness.

I see so many people who try to "go it alone" with the shame and pain of addiction or other family dysfunction. I work with the ones who are ready and willing to share their pain with others, and I pray for the rest. And I pray for myself that I will maintain my own recovery each day. I thank my Higher Power for what has happened in my life since my recovery began. But I no longer try to rescue people. I finally learned that we each must first choose to rescue ourselves. Then others will be there to help.

I am grateful to my mother for the dignity with which she faced the last year of her life, because it reaffirmed my faith that it is never too late to grow. With my father peacefully at rest, she faced her fear and loneliness. On a visit weeks before she died, she looked up from her bed and in a weak but calm voice said that she was ready to die, that she was not afraid. She did a good job of dying. She died well.

What Do Sons Need From Their Mothers?

I watch Linda and David interact every day and I think about mothers and sons. David is a typical 15-year-old and he and Linda have some typical mother-teenager interactions. Of course, neither Linda nor I are perfect parents by any means, just ask our kids. But I am always struck by the healthy things in their relationship that I didn't have in my relationship with my mother. If I could talk to my mother today to tell her what I needed from her when I was a little boy, I would tell her to have her own life, not so we kids would be neglected, but enough that she wasn't disappointed. I would thank her for all the good things that she did, like I thanked her before she died. I would want her to be whole and fulfilled and not to try to get all of her needs met by being a mom. I would want her to go to AA and ACoA meetings, to have friends and support for all of the pain that she grew up with and had in her marriage. I would want her and my father not just to go to three sessions of counseling, but to go until they worked out a big chunk of their pain. I would want her to be powerful but not manipulative. I would want her to keep her sense of humor, but not use it to express anger. I would want her to share her problems with my father and other adults, but not me.

Believe it or not, one of the best things I learned from my father and mother was how to enjoy the company of a partner in life. When my parents were getting along well, which was quite often later in their 51-year marriage, they truly enjoyed talking with each other. Even as a teenager I saw my father come home from work, kiss my mother, and chat away with my mother at the dinner table about their day. Now, no matter where Linda and I are, we spend a chunk of time every day chatting with each other about our respective days.

If I am traveling during the week as I am known to do, we use the telephone a lot. If one of us has clients in the evening, we talk for a couple of hours afterwards. It is one of the best things about a relationship, to have someone who cherishes you and is sincerely interested in who you are and how you feel. I am grateful to my father and mother for that.

I believe that sons need much the same thing from mothers as daughters need from fathers. We need our mothers to be themselves, to reveal themselves to us in appropriate ways and to be role-models for healthy wives or partners. We need our mothers to be powerful but not abusive, and to be vulnerable without being weak. We need them to have healthy relationships with men, to stand up to men when men are abusive or seductive.

I love the fact that Linda is powerful in our relationship, that we respect each other when we are strong and when we are vulnerable. We need our mothers to love us but not to need us as partners. We need them to celebrate when we grow up and leave home, but not to be jealous and angry when we fall in love with our own partner. We need to know of their fear or shame without having to carry it for them. In other words, sons need mothers who are adult women.

I am grateful and happy to see Linda, a grown woman, be a part of David's life. By being a part of *this* family system, I have been allowed to heal some huge childhood wounds. I know that my parents did not have the wonderful opportunities for family recovery that people have today. I am sad for that, but I no longer have to be angry, ashamed or afraid about it. Every father and mother gets dealt a hand in life, and the hand is never perfect. I just hope that Linda and I can continue to grow up and grow old gracefully as we watch our daughters and son begin to be grown up too.

Female Dependency: From Offender- Little Boys To Real Men

WHAT IS AN OFFENDER-LITTLE BOY?

One of the most important aspects of men that was highlighted by the Women's Movement of the '70s was that many of us were raised to be what I call Offender-Little Boys. This label may jar some of you. It is a strong term. But I really can't think of a better one. A lot of women began to feel angry when they saw their husbands pull into the driveway at the end of the day. Women started to exclaim, "Having a husband is like having another child!" A lot of men gave those helpless, blank stares in response. "I'm not dependent," we sputtered. "Look at all I do out in the real world. How can you call me dependent? A baby? Preposterous." And so it went.

Men dug in their heels and denied they had been raised to be dependent on women. Women kept getting sicker of raising their husbands. Men kept denying. Then women started presenting their husbands with divorce papers. Men were astonished, hurt and secretly terrified.

What is an Offender-Little Boy? It is someone who is pretty vulnerable and weak on the inside and destructively powerful on the outside. There are several different male variations of this, and of course, there are female versions as well.

1. Tough Guys

I have worked with many men who are tough, macho, domineering and overtly abusive with women. Inside they are filled with fear and shame. The thought of living on their own, taking care of themselves or being without a woman is overwhelmingly scary. This type of man is the guy we see on the evening news, being shoved into the back of a squad car after beating up or killing the woman in his life. Later, he sobs in court, "I loved her so much. I did it because I loved her."

Guys, we need to face up to some cold, hard realities here. Killing someone, battering them, badgering and beating them with words, constantly frightening them, always hurting their feelings and always overwhelming them because of superior physical strength or debating skills have nothing at all to do with love. Tough Guys hurt women because Tough Guys are terrified of being alone. Fear of abandonment. Fear of not being mothered. Tough Guys hurt women because of severe female dependency. And abusive women hurt men because of severe male dependency.

2. Smart Guys

A more sophisticated version of the Tough Guy is the Smart Guy who manipulates, dominates and overwhelms with his intellect. His superior fire-power comes from verbal debate, analytic thinking and reasoning, logic and suppression of emotion. A Smart Guy can convince a less-than-healthy woman that the sky is green, the sun is blue and that she is dumb even though she has a Ph.D. in astrophysics.

"Honey," he states calmly and rationally, "don't you think our daughters should do all of the chores so that our sons can be involved in football this year?" His wife looks puzzled, and then he adds, "Let's face it. The '60s are over. We agreed that we didn't want our sons to become wimps. Look at all the guys out there who can't stand up for themselves."

His voice takes on a subtle firmness and displeasure at the end of the sentence. His wife gets lost in the logic and in the fear of his becoming more angry. She decides it isn't a big deal anyway, then she agrees with him.

I've seen many a Smart Guy alcoholic convince a very intelligent woman that he isn't alcoholic — he just drinks massive amounts of alcohol because he's not happy with her. I've seen many a Smart Guy convince a very intelligent woman that she has to "put out sexually for him" (a very crude, demeaning way to state it in the first place) all the time because it's the best way for him to feel close, intimate and nurtured. I've seen many a Smart Guy convince his wife and friends that he isn't having an extra-marital affair, when in fact he is. "Smart" is one of the oldest cons in the world.

3. Seductive Guys

Some might argue that this is a variant of Smart Guys or vice versa. Seductive Guys are very powerful, very dangerous and very scared inside. A lot of men who "make it big" by becoming televangelists or the like are actually unrecovering sexual addicts who are very good at seducing not only women, but also large audiences of people. Elmer Gantry isn't alone. He has been joined by Jimmy Swaggart, Jim Bakker and a "heavenly" host of others who can reach right through your television set, into your wallet and leave you begging for more. Sexual seduction always seems to be a part of the act.

There are Seductive Guys right in your own backyard. Recovering sex addicts know they can't "spill their guts" to women because this is one of the best ways to seduce a woman. Women *love* a man who has feelings, right? Many male sex addicts speak with a soft gentle voice, have an endearing boyish aspect to their personalities and can look a woman in the eye and pour out their tales of woe without even a flicker of guilt. A lot of them are great at crying, too, which is a convincing embellishment to the con. After he's "finished" with this woman, he'll leave her in a heap of shame, wondering what she did wrong, when the only mistake she made was to get involved with him in the first place.

Inside of this very powerful Seductive Guy lies an angry wounded little boy who wants to get back at women for all of the hurt that Dad and Mom caused him. Inside is also an extremely lonely little kid who believes that nurturing can only come through his genitals. As men get into recovery from being Seductive Guys, they find that they can actually have self-esteem that is based on who they are rather than on who they can use. They also find that they can have fulfilling, enduring relationships with women without having to be seductive all the time.

An Offender-Little Boy is a man who isn't really a man. Outside he looks mature, whole, intelligent and strong. Inside, he is feeling terrified, desperate and insufficient. Whenever a woman tries to become her own person with her own beliefs, friends, career, ideas or the like, this boy-man will rise up and try to crush her in the hopes that he can keep her in the role that he needs so desperately — wife/mother. The way in which he tries to control and dominate her determines the type of offender he will become.

THE MAKING OF AN OFFENDER-LITTLE BOY

From Dad, we learned to hate women because our fathers had a love/hate (dependency/hate) relationship with our mothers. We learned to do what Dad did. A lot of us were harmed by our fathers, seeing them hurt and overpower our mothers. We learned to belittle women, make fun of women, see women as sex objects, see women as inferior and use women because that's what Dad did. From Dad, we also learned a lot of self-destructive patterns. We learned not to take care of ourselves. We learned not to find nurturing from friendships. We learned not to have feelings. We learned not to value rest, relaxation, compromise, cooperation and inner peace. These hurts keep us little inside. They keep us from growing up.

From Mom, we learned some of the same things but from a different angle. If your mom did all of your laundry, all of your ironing, always handled your social schedule for you, reminded you to wear your coat all the time, never let you make mistakes or hurt — in other words, if she over-mothered you — then you will be fiercely female dependent when you grow up. As an adult, you will probably figure out that you have to move out of the house but when you do, the first piece of "furniture" you'll want to get is a wife. You'll be confused because you'll want her to be independent, witty, intelligent, tireless, always eager to party and travel and whatever, but you'll also demand that she do all the laundry, bear a pack of children for you and raise them single-handedly, work full-time to supplement your income but not make more money than you do and when she is ready to have a nervous breakdown because of this impossible stress, you'll call her "crazy." That's Offender Stuff.

You'll want a woman to nurture you, leave you alone, run your household and wipe your tired brow at the end of the day, but in a flash, she'll be gone. Then the "Dad" in you will lash out in one of the three forms outlined above. You'll beat her physically, verbally or seductively. And the two of you will be miserable.

HOW CAN YOU CHANGE?

It takes a huge amount of courage to admit one or more of these patterns. As in the case of addictions, many of us must be on the verge of total destruction before we'll admit it. But I see men admitting these patterns and growing beyond them day in and day out. It is one of the true joys of my job. So how does a man begin to change?

You must admit that "love by overpowering or manipulation" isn't love at all. You must admit that when you are alone, without a woman, you are scared and you want to become addictive by drinking, smoking, eating, being compulsively sexual and so on. As with all change, *the first step is to admit the problem.* I must say to myself:

First, I am not all grown up. I can't survive on my own. I need women too much, and when they can't meet all of my needs (which is impossible for anyone), I get angry and want to punish them. This stance of mine hurts my wife/lover, it hurts my children and it degrades me. I am ashamed and embarrassed. I need help. I want help. I will now seek help.

Second, I must find help, commit to getting help and begin getting help, so that I can say that as of right now I will do what I need to do to stop hurting those around me.

The moment we take this second frightening descent into self-awakening, we stop being Offender-Little Boys and we start becoming Men. In men's therapy groups, this is one of the most wondrous moments that I am privileged to witness. The "help" to which I refer includes therapy groups, individual therapy, support groups such as AA, Al-Anon and Parents Anonymous, among others. A man must commit to change. Commitment means behavior change, not just repeated apologies and empty promises.

Third, I must own my past mistakes and Offender Behavior. This is a painful yet very simple process of saying to others when appropriate, "I hurt you when I manipulated you into having sex with me when you weren't in the mood, and I am sorry that I hurt you." There must be no if's, and's or but's when this is done. And the other person must be allowed to have their tears or rage, relief, sadness and hurt.

"I hurt you when I hit you, and I am sorry that I did it. It was not okay for me to hit you. I know that I overwhelmed you with logic and made you feel stupid. You are not stupid. And I am very sorry that I did that" To have reverence for your own and the other person's dignity, *do not beg for forgiveness at this time.* To everything there is a season, and this is not the time for begging. Little kids beg and whine when they don't get what they want instantly. Healthy adults know that there is a time to ask, a time to listen, a time to fight for what you want and a time to wait patiently for what you want; a time to explain, and a time to own up and be quiet.

Fourth, I need to get myself into a fiercely rigorous recovery program which includes ongoing support from others outside of my household, ongoing self-care activities and ongoing checks and balances around my past mistakes. A Tough Guy needs to be around folks who will support and nurture him but also demand in friendship that he stop being an Offender. A Smart Guy needs the same thing, as does a Seductive Guy. They need people who care but who won't hang around very long if the Offender Behavior continues unchecked.

Fifth, I need to begin the very rewarding challenge of growing up. This means that I start learning all of the skills and beliefs which define healthy adulthood. I face my childishness, helplessness and female dependency head-on. I look myself in the mirror and say, 'I didn't learn to be a man from my family. I will now accept the challenge of growing up. I *will* become a man.'

BECOMING A REAL MAN

Here's the 64 million dollar question. Now that I've owned up to my lack of maturity and my female dependency, how do I become a man? For one thing, it does *not* mean going to the other extreme and becoming a he-man woman-hater. It does not mean keeping women out of our lives. It does not mean having only male friends.

Becoming a man means nurturing our *inter*dependency. We need to learn to do a lot of new things that we expected women to do for us so that we can then enjoy sharing a much deeper relationship with men and women. If my primary reason for having a woman in my life is to take care of my childhood needs, what room will there be for us to share something deeper like friendship, intimacy, values and true love? There won't be any room for these at all. When my wife walks into the room, I will see a cook, a maid, a chauffeur for me and my children and a mommy who will always make me safe when the world gets scary.

On the other hand, as a man in an adult relationship with a woman, I will see a friend and companion. I will see a very separate adult who has the freedom to leave at any time, but who chooses to be with me because we enjoy each other. I won't see a waitress who brings me my coffee or a seamstress who darns my socks. I'll see a woman who enriches my life because she is a whole and unique adult. The magic in our relationship will always be there because neither of us has control over the other. There will always be that subtle uncertainty and dynamic tension that keep adult relationships fresh, strong and alive. Not the kind of horrible fear-ridden tension that keeps dependent relationships destructive. I mean the healthy tension and uncertainty that all mature adults value and cherish. Having ultimate control over another human being is nothing less than domination and slavery.

Learning Maintenance Skills

Becoming an adult male means that I have to learn those maintenance skills that I never learned. If you learned these, then you're one step closer to being a man. If you haven't, then here is your next challenge. You need to learn:

- *Basic cooking and meal-planning.* Many men and women don't know how to do this. As a result, we eat a lot of junk, a lot of fast food and never have the sense of "home" that comes with a home-cooked meal. Meal preparation is more than just providing calories to burn. The rituals of food preparation help to make a house a home. The smells of stew cooking in a crock pot and the sight of fresh asparagus arranged tastefully on a dinner plate do as much for our psyches as they do for our body cells. This meal preparation is also what many men define as "mothering." What better way to become less female dependent than to learn to do this for yourself.

- *Washing and ironing.* These are more "mom-behaviors." You need to know how to run a washer and dryer, which clothes to do by hand, how to separate them before washing and how to iron them without ruining them. Then you won't feel lost and devastated when the woman in your life goes out of town on business for three days.
- *Cleaning.* Many depressed or stressed people let their "house-hygiene" go to pot; but so do many men who are otherwise functioning pretty well. Taking pride in one's surroundings is the sign of someone with good self-esteem. It also means that other people will be more likely to visit you the next time you invite them, instead of leaving your home in disgust with a vow never to return.
- *Basic sewing skills.* You need to learn how to sew a button on your shirt and how to mend a rip in your jeans. You need to learn this because someday your button will fall off and there won't be a woman there to do it for you. If the button is off your pants, you will either have to sew it back on or let your pants fall down.
- *Basic home repair.* Even though this is usually a "man's job," not all men know how to do this stuff. There's nothing to be ashamed of if you don't know how. You can learn it. The quickest way to learn how to fix a leaky toilet or sink drain is to ask someone who knows. You won't want to do this if you have a lot of shame about yourself, but I highly recommend that you do it this way. People love to look smart by helping. They really don't mind. It took me years to risk asking, but now I wouldn't do it any other way. Experts know all the little tricks that make the job quicker and

easier. Linda loves it when I ask an expert because she used to call me "goop and widget man," in reference to the way I used to jerry-rig everything that I fixed. To be honest with you, she loves it even more when I call a repairperson.

Self-Care And Self-Nurturing

If you can already do the maintenance stuff mentioned above, then the next thing to look at are self-care and self-nurturing behaviors.

Back in 1975, after my first marriage ended and I was in the throes of living alone and trying to feel as if I hadn't lost my grip on life, I realized that I hadn't the foggiest idea about self-nurturing. I was a typical guy. I kept my apartment neat, though not always clean. I went to work everyday. I took care of my kids when they were with me. But something very important was missing. I thought it was a woman. I thought it was "the feminine touch" in my life. But I found that I couldn't just go out and make the "perfect" woman appear at my doorstep, ready to nurture me, give me a backrub, mother me, make my apartment feel "homey" and all the rest.

I finally grew tired of waiting. I also decided that I was tired of needing a woman to do all of that nurturing. Then it hit me like a bolt of lightning! Women were known for their ability to nurture themselves. I had read that in much of the feminist literature. I also realized that I was angry at women because they had something I thought only they could give. I thought that I was helpless! I realized that a lot of it was stuff that I could do for myself. I watched what women did. I read how they took care of themselves. I was intrigued by the notion that all of the primping and preening and bathing and makeup and facials that women did for themselves actually served a very powerful nurturing function.

Pretty early in the game, I figured out that I didn't have to wear makeup to nurture myself. I also figured out that there were many things that I could do that would be okay.

- *Decorating.* I noticed that many women created a sense of home in their apartments and houses by decorating them. They hung pictures on the walls. They bought small pieces of artwork for their coffee tables. They bought themselves flowers, arranged them and then put them on the kitchen table to brighten up the house. So I started to collect decorations for my surroundings. At first the pictures were just nice posters and the artwork a piece of pottery. But over the months and years, my house started to look more like a home. More important, it started to feel like a home.

  The big bonus was that as I experimented with what I liked and didn't like in decorations for my home, I discovered I was also beginning to define more clearly who I was. I learned why our "wants" and "likes" are what make us unique. I learned how they define us as separate from others. We all have needs that are universal, but what we like says who we are to a large degree. (Yes, our beliefs and values also define us. We'll get to those later.) Most of all, it felt good to finally be making a statement about who I was. I was making choices. I was putting my stamp on my surroundings. It started to feel like a home.

- *Nurturing.* We men are not always very kind to ourselves. In "the old days" I would fill my summer days with teaching a graduate class, followed by jogging two to five miles, followed by playing a couple of sets of tennis, followed by an early dinner with friends, followed by chain-smoking cigarettes and downing up to a pint of hard liquor and followed by going to sleep and starting all over again the next day. That was extremely self-destructive behavior. When something was particularly painful, like a crazy relationship, I would simply do more of the same in the hopes of drowning out the pain. Then one day when I was feeling particularly lonely and hurting from something that had happened, I went home, filled the bathtub up, put on some soothing music and just relaxed. What a revelation!

  "This is how those women do it," I thought. "I've finally tapped into one of their great secrets" There are a lot of nurturing things that men can do. We can take hot baths. We can listen quietly to music. We can make a cup of hot tea and read a good book for a while. We can file our fingernails, iron a clean shirt carefully for the next day, meditate and all kinds of things. And we can do these things without giving up one ounce of our masculinity. We just have to do it.

There's another benefit to self-care. In general, people, especially female people, notice things like that. Many women are absolutely turned off by a man who has long, unkempt fingernails or a man who doesn't bathe regularly. I don't blame them. Lack of self-care is a sign that something isn't going well in a person's life. It starts to reflect on one's dignity and self-esteem. It starts to push others away. And as people move away from us, we feel even lonelier than we did before. Self-care is very important.

Support And Friendship Skills

Along with taking care of our bodies, we need to take care of our hearts and souls. Human beings can't function well in prolonged isolation, and men are human beings. So we also need to start cultivating friendships and support.

In *An Adult Child's Guide To What's "Normal,"* Linda and I wrote a lot about the many kinds of friendship that humans need. In overcoming female dependency and in becoming a man, it is crucial that we find more than one source of support in our lives. Putting "all of our eggs in one basket" is very dangerous to ourselves and to the person on whom we rely. We discuss this in depth in our first book, *Adult Children: The Secrets Of Dysfunctional Families.* What happens to most men is that we tie up all of our nurturing needs in one relationship, whether it be a romantic relationship or a friendship. Because it is impossible for one person to meet all of our needs, the relationship eventually collapses under the weight of this impossible demand.

Cultivating friendships is a unique valuable skill that takes time to learn. At first I wanted all of my "support people" to be a carbon-copy of me. I wanted them to like the exact same things, believe the exact same things, feel the exact same things and do the exact same things. Only gradually through the early years of my recovery did I learn that this was hopelessly unrealistic. I learned that what I was looking for were friends who would let me return to the safety of the womb. And that's not possible.

Through AA, therapy groups and my initial clumsy attempts at forming new friendships, I discovered that if I wanted to have people in my life, I was going to have to bend a little. Then I discovered that I would have to bend a lot. And now I have several longstanding friends whom I cherish and value deeply. They are men and women who in some cases are *very* different from me. Some are people with whom I share a hobby, some an idea, some a belief, some a career interest and some share recovery. They are friends and support because we have something in common, we have clear boundaries with each other and we meet a need in each other.

AND NOW?

I began this chapter with an inflammatory label — Offender-Little Boys. I then went on to outline some of the things we need to do to grow up and be men. In closing, I want to make sure that you see the connection between the two.

Let's look at Bill. He used to be a scared, angry little boy in a man's body. He manipulated women, he loved them and hated them. He would lose his temper and hurt them with words. He got them to mother him. He dumped them or they dumped him. His life was a mess. Then he started his recovery. He admitted that he was needy. He admitted that he needed help. He found help. He began to grow up. He learned to take care of himself. He learned to cook, clean, sew, decorate his house, take care of his personal hygiene and be kind to himself when he was feeling vulnerable.

Then Bill developed a solid support network so that when he and a woman broke up, he wasn't terrified or desperate. He was sad, hurt and felt down, but he wasn't paralyzed. He had more than one source of support. He had more than one anchor in his life. He dated women now, rather than trying to "score" or get married immediately. He learned what he liked in a woman and what he didn't. He became more and more whole. He was able to be vulnerable but not defenseless in his relationships. Consequently, the men and women whom he attracted into his life space became healthier and healthier. His unhealthy relationships began to leave his life space. Finally one day he met a pretty darned healthy woman; they fell in love gradually and lived happily ever after.

We were having dinner a few years ago with Minneapolis aerobics expert Gretchen Kellogg. During a discussion of different kinds of therapy that we've known she stopped at one point, thought for a few moments and then declared, "I know the best form of brief psychotherapy around. It's called *grow up!*" And that's the rest of the story.

10

Once Upon
A Time

Once upon a time there was a little boy who lived in a small town out in the middle of nowhere or so it seemed. On crisp spring mornings he would walk to school with a hop and a skip, his heart warming like the ground beneath his feet, his spirit filled with anticipation of the approaching summer. As the daffodils and tulips strained to peek out from the safety of their beds, the little boy would kick a can in front of him all the way down the blacktop street, its music accompanying the quiet symphony of spring. Clatter! Bang! Clink! Clatter! Bang! Rattle! Clatter! The sound of the can rolling and flipping and spinning down the street played with the rhythms of his heartbeat and he was understood.

Excited to learn and to meet other people, the little boy would take his seat in his classroom at school and look up toward his teacher with a freshly-washed face, newly-ironed shirt and trousers, and bright sparkling eyes. His teacher looked out at all of the faces in the room and smiled warmly. Another first grade class was getting ready to finish up and move into the magic of summer — vacations, work on the farm, swimming in the pond, catching frogs and snakes, building forts. It seemed like forever before school would be out for the summer. And as summer progressed, it seemed like forever before school would start again in the fall. Time travels that way for little boys.

It was this way for some time, and then something began to change inside of the little boy. Somewhere along the line he began to learn the world of adults. He did very well in school, which pleased everyone. He hardly ever got into fights. He learned to be nice and to please others and was especially rewarded for this by his parents and teachers. When he was angry, he kept it to himself or he got rid of it by exercising his imagination. He had a wonderful imagination and used it to create fantastic scenarios that made the reality around him much more tolerable. He worked harder and harder in school. His family rewarded him more and more. Overall he felt pretty smug.

He also felt more and more anxious inside. He felt trapped. Restless. He didn't know why. He exercised his imagination more. He tried to please more. But the adults in his world couldn't give him any more attention than they were already giving him. They'd reached their capacity, whatever that was. But the tension inside of him just kept building and building and building until he thought he might burst from the inside out.

The little boy was getting older now. He started to hang around with some kids at school who weren't so nice. He liked being with these boys. They were different. They didn't always follow the rules, which was exciting. They introduced him to smoking which he hated at first but then grew to enjoy more than just about anything.

Later he and his group of friends began to get drunk now and then, and that was *really* fun. Once they shot out some streetlights in the little town. They got caught by the local sheriff because they had bragged about their exploits at school and someone had squealed on them. But generally they were good kids.

The little boy kept his grades up and continued to be the picture of sunlight and perfection around the adults in his world, so the adults continued to smile down upon him with favor. In high school, no one knew that he was a tight bundle of raw nerve endings because on the outside he was always so happy-go-lucky, just like he had been when he first walked down the street and kicked the can on sunny spring mornings. No one knew that he couldn't wait until weekends came so that all of the terrible tension inside of him could be released by getting gloriously, euphorically drunk.

Weekend after weekend he did this, and each time he drank he would feel the warmth and comfort of a lazy sunny summer afternoon enter his body and stay there until the next morning, when he would awake in pain from the damage the alcohol had done to him.

The little boy was almost an adult now and secretly took pride in his double life. He had been living this way for so long that it was second nature to him. He had convinced himself long ago that he was the captain of his own ship, that he was in charge of his own destiny, that whatever good things he did were all up to him and that whatever bad things he did were also all up to him. He didn't know that many of the things that happen to a child are beyond a child's control. Like every child, he blamed himself for anything that went wrong in his life, even when he was a very little child.

The little boy was clever. As a young man he was clever, too. He grew up, fell in love, started a family and tried to become an important adult. But there was always something missing in his life. He always felt as if he was split in two, and he always woke up with hangovers.

Life wasn't much fun any longer. In fact, it hadn't been fun for a long time.

Then one day he met a magical person while he was at work. The man he met lived in a magical way, and the young man said that he wanted to live that way, too. He began to watch the magical man, who finally said to him, "I'm not really a magical man. You want me to be, but I'm not. I'm just a recovering alcoholic who's trying to make the best of his life day-by-day. If you want to have what I have, just work this program of recovery along with me and all of my fellows, then you can have it too."

The young man did just that, and some of the magic began to rub off on him. It was really hard work at first, this "recovery stuff," but it finally started to pay off. Something else began to happen as well. As the young man grew older and he continued to work his recovery program, he began to heal the wounds that had happened to him as a child — that had caused him to split into two parts, that weren't his fault, for which he always blamed himself, many of which he did not even know were wounds when they first happened. The more they healed, the more the two parts of himself started pulling together. The more they pulled together, the more whole he felt. The more whole he felt, the more healthy he was. "This is a neat system," he thought to himself. "This is so cool!"

Then something truly magical happened. It was on a crisp spring morning. He had got up early to take his dog for a walk. His wife and children were still asleep, safely tucked in their beds. He walked across the big open field behind his house and down onto the blacktop road that meandered along the lake. The geese honked a brassy "good morning" to him. His dog chased a squirrel. The early morning sun sparkled and glittered among the budding green oak leaves as a lone puff of wind caused them to flutter. He felt whole inside.

As he looked down at the ground that was beginning to warm up after the long cold winter, he saw it there. Slightly crumpled, somewhat worn, but the label still legible — it was a can! A twinkle came into his eye. His heart fluttered for a moment. And then he zeroed in on that can like a pitcher about to deliver the last pitch of a no-hitter in the last game of the World Series. His foot went back, and with all of his might, he kicked that can clear down the blacktop street.

With a hop and a skip, with his heart warming like the ground beneath his feet, his spirit filled with anticipation of the approaching summer, and with a smile on his face that reflected back the strengthening rays of the sun, he continued down the road. The daffodils and tulips strained to peek out from the safety of their beds as the man kicked the can in front of him all the way down the blacktop street, its music accompanying the quiet symphony of spring. Clatter! Bang! Clink! Clatter! Bang! Rattle! Clatter! The sound of the can rolling and flipping and spinning down the street played with the rhythms of his heartbeat, and he was understood.

4

HOPE,
HEALING
AND
HONOR

All things are connected like the blood which unites one family. Whatever befalls the earth befalls the sons of the earth.

Chief Seattle
1854

11

Healing Our
Father Wound

MEMORIES

At the present time I am very grateful. I am 43 years old. I am in my office at my home in St. Paul, Minnesota. It is 10 degrees below zero outside. The bright low afternoon sun plays magic with the pine trees outside my window. The ground is covered with six inches of newly fallen, powdery snow. My trusty dog, Nik, a yellow Labrador and German Shepherd mix who looks a bit like Old Yeller is snoozing downstairs in the kitchen. David, 15, is watching a Minnesota Vikings football game. Linda is out doing some last minute Christmas shopping. My daughters will be coming home Christmas Eve and we will all be leaving Christmas morning for a family vacation to a warm climate for 10 days.

On the bookcase behind me are mementos from my childhood in California — my Little League baseball cap, a papier mache camel that I made in the first grade, a photograph of my Little League team, shells that I collected at Stinson Beach, a Swiss Army knife, some duck calls, one of my father's old watches that hasn't worked for years and a few other things from more recent eras in my life.

On the wall of my office are pictures of my three children at various ages, pictures of my brother, sister, father, mother and me, and three of my favorite pictures of Linda and me. There is a picture of me on my brother-in-law's fishing boat off the coast of Catalina Island. I have a fighting belt around my waist and am holding up a small shark that I caught. I have yet to catch a marlin, but I like the times that Bill and I spend on the boat. The marlin really don't matter. Bill releases all the ones that he catches now anyway.

I am always moved when I look at the picture of my sister, brother and me standing together in our jeans and T-shirts on a summer vacation somewhere. I am about six in the picture. Our vacations were a curious mix of magic and enmeshment, sadness and excitement. The one of me at age two, on the sand of Stinson Beach, covered with cold salt water, a towel wrapped around me, licking the salt from my upper lip, is one of my favorites. I no doubt was freezing and about to race back into the whitewater for "just one more" tumble in the surf before actually getting out for a while to warm up.

As my eyes move across the wall and onto the corner of the desk, they fall on a nice clutter of pictures in frames — some short, some tall, some in front and some behind. Kristin and Rebecca, about ten and seven, their hands on the head of their now-departed English sheepdog, Agatha, smile out into the room. David, about five, looks dapper and innocent in his plaid shirt and grey sweater. I can feel tears of pride and relief well up in my eyes when I consider what extraordinary people they are becoming. Not saints, mind you, but truly marvelous human beings. My favorite picture of Linda, from before we were married, lights up the room with her grace and joy still clearly evident in a faded 35mm print. The picture of my parents with Kristin and Rebecca is warm.

And then, behind all the rest and much larger, too, is the picture of my father a couple of years before he died. Part of him looks just like any other old man who has had a stroke. He has on baggy trousers, a T-shirt and an old cardigan sweater that is open and hanging loosely from his shoulders. In his left hand is the bamboo cane that he used to steady himself. On his face is permanently sculpted the enthusiasm and liveliness of a teenager. It isn't really the picture that's larger than the others. It's just that he projected a presence that was larger than life, right up until the day that he died.

He was such a paradox. The frightened part of him was so destructive and the spiritual part of him was so touching. His moments of vulnerability were very moving, very subtle and too few and far between. On several occasions, especially when I was young, he would tell the story of the time that he nearly died from fever when he was a little boy. At the moment his fever began to break, he said that he saw an angel floating back and forth before his eyes reassuring him that, "All is well. All is well."

It reminds me of a time not too long ago, after he had died, when I was fretting and stewing in fear about paying bills. Linda and I awoke one morning and she turned to me with an unforgettable look of wonder in her eyes and said, "Your dad just came into my dream and said 'Tell John to relax. He has all that he needs.' " Was it really him? Was it Linda hoping that I would relax? It doesn't matter. I have never forgotten that morning. My father liked Linda.

He worried when we children hurt, even though he caused a lot of that hurt himself. Whenever I feel that survival fear, which was *his* greatest fear as well, I hear those words, say the Serenity Prayer and let go of the fear again.

I look at the face in that picture on my desk and I see a man who tried very hard to be a good father, who failed miserably in some ways but who achieved success in many other ways. I look at that face and I feel a deep sadness that he and my mother didn't have the same recovery resources that I have now. I feel joy and excitement, for he was a joyous and exciting person. I feel traces of anger as I reflect on the damage that he did. And I feel a deep peace, too. He lived a full life. His fear of surviving is now over. He faced the debilitation of his stroke during the last seven years of his life with dignity, mostly. During the last three years or so, I watched in amazement as he lived inside of an aphasic brain and a partially paralyzed body, bedridden much of the time, but always somehow able to maintain his spirit and his sense of humor. He knew who Linda was but most of the time he couldn't remember her name due to his stroke. As we would be leaving for the airport after visiting, he would struggle to say goodbye to her. "Where's that girl?" he would finally blurt out in barely understandable muttering. I would ask, "Do you mean 'Linda'?" And he would laugh with relief and shout, "Yes!" I would call Linda in and he would give her a big smile and try to say the word "goodbye."

He was too scared to speak of his own death, which makes me sad. On one of my visits to California I brought up the subject but he quickly changed it. I was in my thirties by then and didn't feel an uncontrollable need to press the issue with him. I figured his death was a personal thing for him. And sure enough, he managed to die a dignified death despite my inability to get him to talk about it beforehand. We all die anyway, you might protest. What did he have to do with it? Well, he did it, that's all. I somehow have a sense that he was okay with it, too, which makes my fear of living and dying much less these days. I thank you for that, Dad.

OF DREAMS AND HEALING

Would it have been better if my father and mother had accepted the gerontological counseling that my sister and I tried to set up for them? Would it have been better if he had been able to heal his wounds with his own father before he died? Or if he had healed some of the deeper wounds with us kids before he died? Yes, it would have been better. But he didn't. What is better is not always what is real. And so most of us men are left with an open wound about our fathers. *As adults, we must take it upon ourselves to do this healing. No one can do it for us.*

I have never seen men react to a movie the way that I saw them react to *Field of Dreams.* Men who claim that they have never cried in their lives told me that they cried freely during this film. It reached down inside of the hearts and souls of thousands of men and said, "I know that you hurt. I know how you hurt. I know that you want to stop hurting. And I believe there's a way to do it." Even if you have already seen the movie once, I encourage you to see it again, and perhaps again after that. It is a beautiful example of how men can relate to each other as men of depth, rather than just as men.

One wonderful aspect of this movie is that it actually gives us a roadmap to this healing if we are willing to let it do so. If you will bear with me for a little while, I'll try to show you what I mean, step-by-step, as we look at this near-perfect "men's film."

The Overt History

Field Of Dreams begins with the kind of overt history we all do at one time in our lives. "I was born on such and such a date. My parents were so and so. We lived in this city or that. I left home as soon as I could and never looked back. I married a wonderful woman. We settled down and raised a family." On and on it goes. My father's father (my grandfather) spent a lot of time in his twilight years putting together a small book documenting these sorts of things for our branch of the Friel family. It is fun to read *The Story Of Edward And Margaret Friel* (Friel, 1948) — of my ancestors coming to America, going across the prairie, establishing a homestead and beginning our family tree. It is even somewhat informative. But it lacks one essential ingredient. It says very little about the covert, emotional reality of our ancestors. These are the realities which we must discover in our own histories if we are ever to become whole adults. It isn't enough to look at our childhoods as if we were reading safely edited entries in an encyclopedia. But this is the first way that a young adult will look at his or her reality.

The "Normal" Life

We go into adulthood leading our "normal" life. We all seem to have similar life structures, well documented now in the work of Levinson and Gould, among others. We start our first adult "dream," fashioned like, or exactly unlike that of our own childhoods. In our 20s and even into our early 30s, we play out a drama that is pretty much scripted by whatever happened to us in childhood. With wide-eyed zeal we go out into the world and try our hand at being adults, leaving behind that part of ourselves which was childhood. And in the process, even the healthiest of us leave parts behind that have yet to heal.

The Magic

And then one day, if we are open to life, we hear a voice that urges us to risk a healing journey. The baseball fields that our inner voices tell us to build are as varied as we are. They all lead us in the same direction — toward a period of inner reflection and deeper discovery of ourselves. And they all have one thing in common. What our voices tell us to do is scary.

The Child

As in *Field Of Dreams*, it is the child in us who sees the magic first. It is the child in us who feels the magic first. It is the child in us who first tries to respond to the magic. It is the child in us who believes in magic. This is why it so important for us to heal our childhood wounds. Until we do, we push that part of ourselves away, never to be able to find the magic in our lives. Magic is much too scary to find until we do so.

The Leap Of Faith

As so many of us find out in recovering from addictions, there is an initial payoff that gives us a sense of euphoria. We quit drinking or using drugs or overeating or over-working and our lives get better fast. But better compared to what? To our earlier life of using. But is there more to life than this? The quick payoff? The easy buck? Nirvana in a minute? Just when we think our mission is accomplished, we find out that it is really just a beginning. This is the core truth beneath any growth or recovery and it requires a huge leap of faith.

The Quest

Our faith is tested. A challenge is posed. It isn't over. It's just beginning. And so we begin our quest, which entails gathering up fragments, bits and pieces from our pasts. But it isn't a quest of time and place and events. It is a quest of the magic and power that makes up our deeper covert reality — the one that makes us human. It is a reality of feelings, of lost dreams, of pain and joy and of dignity. It is a quest for our lost selves. A search for those parts of childhood tucked neatly away in the backs of our minds as we zealously went into the world to become adults.

The men with whom I work every week in group know just exactly what this quest is about. They face the same nagging doubts, the same exhilaration followed by disappointment. I watch them and share with them as they begin to gather up the bits and pieces of their childhoods, feel feelings for the first time, get scared and back off, encounter resistance from their friends and family, then get right back in and do some more work. I watch as the magic unfolds for each one of them, each in his own way, each on his own quest; just like in the movies.

I watch their family members, too. I see them excited at first. And then doubting. Then angry and disappointed. Then excited again. If they choose to, these family members begin to let their own magic unfold in the same way. I don't need to go onto a battlefield to see courage and valor. I see it every day at work. For that, too, I am grateful.

The Showdown

With all of the players back at the ballfield, the show-down begins. The critical moment of truth arrives. All of the work that made up the quest comes to bear in one critical moment. And by believing that the moment has arrived before it actually has, many of us jump the gun and try to take what isn't meant to be ours. If we do this, we never get what it is we are supposed to get.

"All this work and recovery and what do I get? My wife just anounced that she's divorcing me. Doesn't she know I've changed? Can't she see it?"

The 11th Step of Alcoholics Anonymous asks us to keep up our faith in a Higher Power, ". . . praying only for knowledge of God's will for us and the power to carry that out." It took me a long time to quit wishing and asking for specifics, to realize that I don't always have the answers. It is a matter of true faith to actively pursue our life goals but to continue to be open to the possibility that what we want right now may not be all that is out there for us.

The Payoff

It is only after months and even years that we truly find what it is we have been searching for. Beauty and depth in life don't come easy. A good, strong father can help his sons learn this lesson. A job isn't finished until it's finished. Taking risks, working hard, having personal integrity, wait-ing, watching and learning, giving mentors their due, pay-ing one's dues, handling disappointment gracefully — these are all things that we can learn from a good strong father. Good therapists know this. We would love to be able to wave a magic wand and make our clients' lives instantly full and healthy. But we know it doesn't work that way. Our clients get angry at us for not saving them. They want solutions when the only ones are inside of themselves. We struggle and watch our clients struggle.

And then something glorious happens. In the movies it all happens in a couple of hours. It seems to happen magically. In real life it happens slowly but in much the same way. The wounds that we carry from our imperfect fathers can run very deep. Getting to them can be hard and painful. But the rewards are just as powerful, just as moving and just as liberating and healing as the emotionally-freeing conclusion to *Field Of Dreams.*

In *Field Of Dreams,* Kevin Costner portrayed a man who took a big gamble as he followed his inner voice. He persevered despite ridicule, others' anger, possible bankruptcy and his own doubts as to his sanity. He demonstrated a kind of faith seldom seen nowadays because the reward that he earned was elusive right up until the very end. It was a "man's film" with a man's backdrop — the game of baseball. It was about a man who listened to an inner voice, who went on a quest, who was willing to risk all to help another man to heal and who was rewarded with the greatest gift of all for a man today — one last chance to heal his Father Wound.

The journey that we must take to become true men is an arduous one. It requires that we demythologize our fathers. We must take them off the pedestals on which we have put them. We must take them out of the gutter in which we have put them. It demands that we go back into our childhoods one last time, as if we are on a search for fire-breathing dragons and demons. It demands that we re-experience the pain of childhood. In the process we must let our fathers become real human beings instead of saints or devils. In the process we must embrace the parts of ourselves that are just like our fathers. We must see how in over-reacting, we have become the very opposite of our fathers in some ways; and in doing so, have created equally painful lives. As we complete this process, we can begin to stop betraying our maleness. We can begin to have true male friends. We can stop apologizing for being men; and we can stop hurting others with our maleness.

We can become powerful men who have humility and gratitude and wisdom and strength.

When I first began my own healing quest back in the 1970s, I ran across the writings of Lao Tsu, the Chinese sage, who is credited with writing the *Tao Te Ching* in the sixth century B.C. These writings express the essence of Taoism, which is similar to the basic principles of Alcoholics Anonymous. This is one of the messages I never forgot. It has helped me to focus my energy and my recovery so that there is follow-through and not just the excitement of beginnings:

> *People usually fail when they are on the*
> *verge of success.*
> *So give as much care to the end as*
> *to the beginning.*
> *Then there will be no failure.*

Lao Tsu
Tao Te Ching
(translated by Gia-Fu Feng and Jane English, 1972)

12

Men In Recovery/Men In Group

There is perhaps nothing sadder and more scary than a man who is unwilling to grow up. By the same token, there is nothing more inspiring and joyous than a man who is willing to sit with other men and say that he needs help. I consider it an honor to watch week after week as the 24 men in my three therapy groups struggle to support each other and to share their pain and joy. I drive home from group at night regardless of what went on, feeling like the luckiest man alive. It is truly a spiritual experience for me. A down-to-earth, honest, hands-dirty, real, spiritual experience. If you were to be a little mouse in the corner of one of the group sessions you might not have any idea why I say that. Some evenings are dramatic enough for you to get a taste of it. But what really happens in group is that a bunch of men who learned to be terrified of their feelings, their vulnerability, their power and each other slowly develop a sense of family connection that only time allows. There is no quick fix for this stuff.

As the weeks progress, old members "graduate" and new members join the group, so that there are hellos and goodbyes just like in a family of origin. But what is different from many families in America is that the rules change. Competent professionals like doctors and attorneys sit with competent craftsmen like plumbers and electricians. Carpenters and laborers sit with teachers and unemployed men. Everyone fits because the goal is not to produce anything tangible, like money. The goal is to heal. Men who have no "real friends" outside of group and see other men as competitors begin to care for each other as equals who have strengths and weaknesses. Weaknesses start to be okay instead of being something to hide. Failures which were once a source of deep shame are seen for what they are — a chance to make decisions and change.

The rule which says that the only feelings men feel are "anger and lust" doesn't hold in group. Men who are angry learn to express their shame and fear. Men who are sad learn to get angry and laugh. Men who are scared learn to find their power. The rule which says that the only way to measure a man's worth is by his income or status doesn't apply either. Everyone comes into group with these rules, but they don't leave with them.

Because this is not a clinical book for professionals, I won't go into depth on techniques or methods. Rather, I will just share a couple of the things we work on in group to give you an idea of what it's about.

IN THE BEGINNING

As the eight men filter into group just before it begins, you might not see much difference between what goes on there and what goes on at a sports club or a social gathering. There is a lot of small talk, laughter, friendly bantering and getting reacquainted. If you could feel the non-verbal communication going on, though, you would even detect a difference at this beginning. There is a subtle respect and concern for each other, a caring, that is different somehow. Members who have been in group for a fairly long time have built up a history with each other, having shared births and deaths, marriages and divorces, laughter and tears. There are clearly relationships there.

When it is time to begin, I give the sign and the talking and laughter abruptly end as everyone gets ready to do their work. The first thing we do is bid for time. This ensures that each person reflects before group about what it is he wants to work on, and roughly how much time he wants to do it in, which puts the responsibility for his work squarely on his own shoulders.

Next we do a feelings check, which means that each person shares with the group how he is feeling right now. Editorializing is not a part of this check. Each man simply says something like, "I'm feeling some anger and some sadness," or "I'm feeling some fear and some shame and some anger," or "I'm feeling very happy and peaceful." A new member sometimes tries to editorialize a lot, as in "I'm feeling scared because my boss or my wife just came down on me pretty hard, and I don't think it will turn out okay, but I've thought about what I'm going to do." I gently break in and pull him back to his feelings, and then we move on to the next person.

This feelings check may sound pretty simple and unimportant, but it is very powerful because it requires us to short-circuit our typical male way of relating. It also grounds us in our feeling reality, where we don't often stay very long. And it grounds us in the here and now, which is where we are.

From then on, each man who has bid for time takes his time. We focus in group on a number of areas, including doing family-of-origin work to help men heal their pasts and see how they are still acting out their pasts in the present. We also deal with present issues that men are struggling with, and we deal with the relationships be-

tween members of the group. We use all kinds of thera-
peutic methods, including gestalt/feelings work, cognitive
restructuring work, insight-oriented therapy, family systems work, psychodrama and the like.

As each man does his work, he is sharing a part of
himself that was previously unshared, which is a gift to
the group. As each man shares his work with the group,
he gets the power of having a witness to his work, and
therefore to himself. As each man listens to the work of
others, he also gets the gift of permission, as well as data
about family and relationships that may have a direct bear-
ing on his own life. It is exciting to see the "lightbulbs of
insight" go off in the other group members as one man
does his work.

FAMILY-OF-ORIGIN WORK

A huge chunk of what men do in my groups is to work
through issues of overt and covert abuse and dysfunction
in their families of origin. An example of some of the kinds
of families in pain I work with are shown in Figure 12.1.

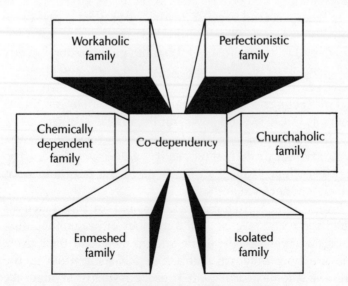

Figure 12.1. Some Families In Pain

I try very often to make it clear that having a painful childhood is not an excuse for hurting self or others in the present. This means that we have to own up to and hold ourselves accountable for the painful things we are doing in the here and now. Then we can hold our families accountable for what happened to us, and then we can let go of the past and move on.

In our first two books, Linda and I present in detail what many of these issues are, so I won't go into detail here. Please realize that this part of the work — untangling our pasts and the hidden patterns that we are still living out — can take a good one to two years depending on what happened in childhood. It can be shorter for some and longer for others, depending on what happened to us as kids.

	Positive Traits	Negative Traits
Father		
Mother		

Figure 12.2. A Close Look At Our Parents

One of the homework assignments that I give around family of origin is to begin listing the positive and negative characteristics of Dad and Mom, which can be a very difficult but revealing exercise. A sample of how to lay this out for maximum awareness of patterns is shown in Figure 12.2. After a man has done this part to his satisfaction, I then ask him to make up the same chart for himself and his partner, if he has one. When he brings all of this data about himself to group, we then put it up on the flipchart so that everyone can see how the patterns have unfolded, and he can get the input of everyone in group. The feedback from the group members can be very affirming, insightful and powerful.

Feelings Work

During family-of-origin work, men have an opportunity to do the cognitive head stuff about understanding intellectually what happened, which is fairly easy for a lot of men. But they also get the chance to do the more difficult feelings work around what happened to them. For most men this is where the big life-breakthroughs come. There is something extremely powerful and honoring about witnessing a man cry with dignity rather than shame and to see other men handle it without squirming, laughing, shaming or running away and turning on the television set. In the beginning it's like pulling teeth for many men. A lot of us learned to be emotionally constipated in our families and it takes some work to get unstuck.

Whether it's anger work from a man who was never allowed to have healthy anger, or grief work from a man who was never allowed to cry with strength and dignity, the feelings part of the work is always a significant experience for everyone. Men work through tremendous guilt and shame about themselves, their feelings and how they have been treated and how they have treated others throughout their lives. They deal with deep sadness and powerful fears of abandonment and loneliness. Each time they do, another part of them heals and their eyes get clearer, their faces look stronger and their lives get better.

The feelings work must end at some point. Some therapists are very skilled at helping people get into their feelings, but then that's all they do. Week after week their clients are doing anger and grief work, but it's as if they get addicted to it after a while. There comes a time when we need to say, *"I have done enough for now. It is time to get on with my life."* To believe that a person cannot be happy until he has purged every last hurt and pain from his past is a setup for never being happy.

Table 12.1. Feelings And What They're For	
Safety/warmth	Okay, needs met
Dependency	Can be own age
Pain	Avoid/recognize damage
Sadness	Heal loss
Pleasure/joy	Uniqueness
Shame	Accountable/spiritual
Guilt	Correct errors
Fear	Wisdom
Lonely	Embrace self
Sexuality	Maleness/femaleness

For those of you not familiar with our work, I have listed in Table 12.1 the basic feelings that we feel, and what the feelings are for. Please remember:

- All feelings are good. There's no such thing as a bad feeling.
- What we do with our feelings can either be bad or good for us. Everyone feels sexual at times. It's what you do with it that matters.
- Feelings are felt in our bodies, not in our foreheads. If you have trouble getting to your feelings, pay attention to your breathing, muscle tension, stomach, back, guts, etc.
- If you are so angry that you can't feel anything, please notice how silly that sounds. Anger is a feeling.
- Please try not to use euphemisms to describe your feelings. Also, try to avoid words that are weak, such as "frustrated," when what you mean is "angry."

Because feelings can be so scary, I try to point out to men the difference between the feeling in its healthy form and the feeling when it gets out of control, as shown in Figure 12.3.

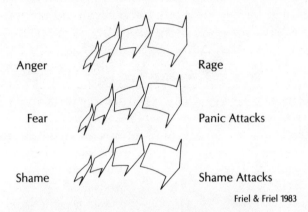

Anger   Rage

Fear   Panic Attacks

Shame   Shame Attacks

Friel & Friel 1983

Figure 12.3. When Feelings Get Too Big

Anger, for example, is appropriate if it is direct, clear and produces constructive changes in one's life.

Rage, on the other hand, is always abusive and should never be foisted on another person. Rage can be okay now and then if you are alone and don't harm yourself, or if you are in a therapy group with a therapist who knows how to do rage work, not just anger work, and if everyone in the group knows how to make themselves safe while you are doing that work.

When *fear* gets too big for us, it becomes a *panic attack,* which can be very debilitating. I had panic attacks for a six-month period toward the end of my first marriage, and I know how scary they can be. If your fear gets this big, please know that the majority of phobias and panic attacks are ultimately treatable without drugs. You may need to be on a mild anti-anxiety agent for a short time while in therapy, but most people can work the panic attacks through after tracing them to a deep-seated fear of abandonment or loss of life that began with childhood abuse or neglect. This work may take what seems like a long time, but it beats getting addicted to Valium or Xanax, which are very dangerous drugs.

Along the same lines, when *shame* gets too big, we have **shame attacks,** in which a man or woman who is perfectly capable suddenly feels like he or she is terribly small, helpless, worthless and useless. If we are feeling tired or down about something and we ask a favor of a friend, but the friend can't help right this minute, we might have a shame attack and blow the whole thing out of proportion.

"Joe can't help me hang my storm windows today. It must be because I'm such a worthless person. Joe must secretly hate me." What I encourage men to do is to identify a shame attack as just that — a shame attack. It helps a lot to do this so that we can keep our feelings in perspective.

Another way to look at the problems we have identifying our feelings is to realize we often hide or cover up one feeling with another. We men are notorious for doing this without vulnerability, but so are many women.

As you look at Figure 12.4, reflect on your own feelings and reactions. Realize that in many interactions with others, we feel more than one feeling. But also note whether or not you do any of this covering up.

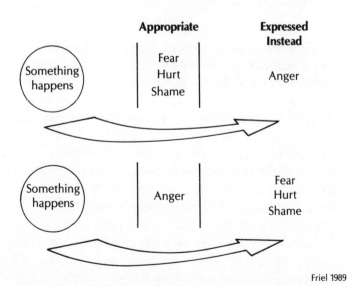

Friel 1989

Figure 12.4. When We Block Feelings With Feelings

For example, if you say that you don't like something about me, or if you get angry at me and start to withdraw from me, it would be normal and appropriate deep inside to feel fear, hurt and shame. But many of us cover these up and mask them by going directly to anger to protect and defend ourselves. Some families have a hidden rule that says, "Don't be vulnerable." That same rule also says, "Hide it all with anger and defensiveness." In the same way, some people have no trouble with their vulnerability at all. In fact, they are too vulnerable all the time and lack the healthy anger necessary to protect themselves. In this case, let yourself feel the fear, hurt and shame, but then let yourself get to your protective anger.

The other thing that I want to say about feelings is that men do not have to express feelings the same way that women do. There is much talk these days about men honoring each other, and I like the concept. There *is* a different way that men affirm each other. Sometimes it is a nod of approval. Sometimes it is with excited agreement. Sometimes it is with a tear. We do not have to be women to be healthy men.

SEXUALITY

There are some excellent resources out on men's sexuality already (e.g., Zilbergeld, 1978; Fossum, 1989), but I do want to say a few things about it here.

For many years I have felt strongly that sexuality is a subset or part of intimacy, and that trying to have intimacy through sexuality, rather than letting sexuality be an expression of intimacy that is already building gets us into trouble ultimately. If we let our sexuality become a tool of medication or replacement for intimacy that isn't there, we only multiply problems in the relationship that need to be looked at.

In some very important ways, our sexuality is a core part of our identity and our spirituality. Whether you are gay or straight, you are also a man or a woman, and this is a part of you that needs to be affirmed and embraced by you. Likewise, our spirituality flows from our self-identity and is an expression of a relationship with something more powerful than ourselves. When we say that a man "has spirit," we are saying that he is alive, is present, isn't afraid to proclaim his identity, and is open to embracing all that is good out there in the universe. When we use our sexuality instead of embracing it, we devalue ourselves and our spirit. It is a big challenge for children to grow up and become adults, and part of this challenge is to come to terms with their sexuality. In America we have some pretty confusing messages that make this challenge particularly hard.

On the one hand, we have a very puritanical view of sexuality deep in our national core so that no matter how open we seem to be on the surface, we still feel more shame about our sexuality than a lot of other nations. On the other hand, we have learned too well that sex can be used to titillate and entice, so we have an opposite but equally dysfunctional view of sex that is used to sell everything from beer to cars to vacations in the Caribbean to water pumps. The recovering sex addicts in my groups know they can act out their addiction by simply looking at the three major T.V. networks or most national magazines — sex is used everywhere to sell stuff, which really cheapens what sexuality is truly about. The double message is thus:

> *Sex is embarrassing and shameful.*
> *Sex is exciting, titillating, and cheap.*

The crucial question then is, "What does it mean to use my sexuality?" We use sexuality when . . .

- It is our *only* method of giving or receiving affection.
- We make objects of others, i.e., we stare at them, visually undress them or fantasize about them, without there being an intimate relationship between us. Or, if this is all we do with a person with whom we are involved.
- We use sex to medicate our feelings, as in compulsively masturbating to treat our loneliness or shame.

- We use sex to resolve fights or conflicts.
- We use sex to avoid other forms of intimacy and communication within the relationship. A couple may make love
  when what they really want to do is to look each other in
  the eyes and say, "I need a little bit of time away from you
  now and then."
- We use sex as a way to manipulate or control another
  person as in using it as a "bargaining chip" in relationship
  negotiations. This is seldom ever overt or spoken. It just
  happens "under the table."

A lot of us men get messages about our bodies that are
not healthy. Some of us get grandiose messages in which
we have the delusion that all women are just dying to get
us into bed, that all women stare at us and imagine us
nude, erect and powerful, and that we therefore have
unlimited license and power to act out our sexuality whenever, wherever and with whomever we choose. Some of
us get inferiority messages, in which we believe that our
bodies are awful, that women are disgusted by the sight
of our penises, whether erect or not, and that sex is just
a dirty necessity.

To like your body and to like your partner's body is
good. To lose yourself in sexual passion with a partner
whom you love is a beautiful, magnificent, spiritual experience. To lose your *self* in a relationship of any kind is
unhealthy. Our sexuality is a part of our soul. Sometimes
it is passionate and intense, sometimes it is warm and
comfortable and silly, sometimes it is "the same" and sometimes it is "unique."

The path to healthy sexuality begins with learning
about ourselves and is therefore about identity development. If we learn to like who we are, "warts and all," then
we have traveled a good way down this trail. Farther on
down, we encounter our relationships with others, which
is called intimacy. This includes who we get along with
and who we don't, how we get our needs met and meet
others' needs and sharing of values. If this part of the trip
goes well, then we become capable of spirituality, which

means that we can have a healthy relationship with the unknowable in the universe. This last step takes a lot of trust, a lot of faith, a lot of hope, a lot of respect, a lot of patience, a lot of courage and the willingness to let go. Of course, these are all necessary for life-enhancing sexuality, so maybe it all makes sense.

AWAKENING MEN

What I have shared in this chapter is just a tiny bit of what men work on in therapy groups and does not do justice to the awe-inspiring work that I see each week. Some things just can't be expressed well in words either, but I believe that their work fits this category.

Many of us who are men try to produce our own physical or emotional deaths through the unhealthy ways we live, and some of us die trying. Others choose a different form of "death" in which we choose to heal the wounds by admitting that we have problems. As we awaken in recovery, we gradually say goodbye to the unhealed parts of ourselves and begin to embrace life. As we risk to share who we really are with other men who are safe, instead of hanging around men who aren't safe, we begin to receive gifts that make our lives exciting and full, not dangerous and awful. As we ride into the battlefield of our own demons, we dare to become men.

I am proud to be a part of that process.

13

Noticing
And
Listening

WHY DO IT?

eing a man can be hard. We are unsure of how to act or of how to be at times. We are trained to act. We are supposed to be decisive. Because of this pressure to act, we sometimes get paralyzed. Or, we act but later regret what we did. At other times we simply don't know what we want. We are unsure. What we fail to see is that there is nothing wrong with being unsure now and then. Put another way, there *is* something wrong with being sure all the time. A man who is sure all the time is either delusional or he is God. I feel safe in assuming that you and I are not God so it must be delusional.

I have worked with many therapists as clients who had the delusion they must always have the answers and they must be invincible, infallible, flawless, tireless and capable of superhuman work hours. I once operated this way also. Now I help my therapist clients to see how trying to be God is a dangerous delusion born out of shame and fear. Most of them eventually get it, which is important because it is important for all human beings, including therapists, to be able to tolerate uncertainty. Without this ability to tolerate uncertainty, we never collect enough information from the world to make good decisions.

Noticing and *Listening* are very important parts of making good decisions. Sometimes when I am unsure of something inside or outside of me, I will stop, put down everything I am doing, sit still and be quiet. This is not something that always came easily to me. It comes fairly easily now. Even a few years ago, if I was uncertain about something, I would shift gears, shove the gas pedal to the floorboard and career headlong into the problem. This strategy worked now and then but I'm not convinced it served me very well over the long haul. It didn't allow me to have much depth.

Mind you, I'm not suggesting every time you have even the smallest decision to make, you drop everything and sit and contemplate your navel for a while. If our wonderful business manager, Arlene, asks if I want to buy a new copying machine from the salesperson on the phone, I can quickly ask, "Is there anything wrong with the one we have?" If she says that it's working fine, then I can quickly say, "No, tell the salesperson we don't need one." That's simple enough. But what if Linda asks me where I would like to go for vacation or how I think we should deal with a problem with one of the kids? What if someone approaches me at a conference and asks if he or she can work in our business with us? What if someone about whom I am unsure invites me to his birthday party? In many of these cases, I will probably do a fair amount of noticing and listening.

How Do You Do It?

Noticing and *Listening* are more passive than they are active, so doing them will invite many men to change their stance in life. Doing them will require that many of you stretch beyond your current capabilities. Realtors use that word "stretch" pretty effectively when they try to get you to take out a mortgage a little bit bigger than you had planned. But with noticing and listening, I don't think you'll have to risk future bankruptcy. You may have to stretch, though. You will also have to practice. This means that you cannot just think that you can change and then automatically change. You really must practice.

Practice Being Still.

One way to begin to develop this skill is to practice being still. It doesn't matter where you do this, which is nice. When I was first teaching this to clients, I would suggest they go outside and sit under a tree for an hour without any distractions. No radio, no notebook, paper or pen. No friends, lovers or pets. Clients came back and said that this was a very hard assignment. They also came back and said that they liked it. That was in the Minnesota summertime when sitting under a tree was feasible. When winter arrived, there weren't many folks who wanted to go sit under a tree at 10 degrees below zero.

Then one day I decided to bundle up and do one of my five-mile jogs around the lake behind my house. I had on two pairs of polpropylene long underwear, a sweatsuit, a face mask, a ski hat over that and the sweatsuit hat over it, a very warm pair of socks and on top of all that, a Gortex running suit and two pairs of gloves. The idea of course is that as you heat up from the run, you can start to shed some of the clothes to adjust your body temperature. Needless to say, I looked silly. Even Nik, my dog, thought I looked silly. He refused to run with me that day, and I know it was due to his embarrassment.

I did the run, which was fine. When I was done, I put back on the clothes I had shed, walked off into the field behind my house, lay down in the snow and was very still for a long time. It was absolutely marvelous! The air temperature was 22 degrees below zero, the wind chill was around 65 degrees below zero, I was comfortably warm and I was outside being very still. It was actually a very spiritual experience. As I recall it now, I was able to notice and listen just enough that afternoon to get the answer I needed to a very knotty problem.

Let In Your Outer And Inner Environments.

Do you have to sit under a tree to do this? Do you have to do it when it's 65 degrees below zero? Nope. You get to find your own place to be still. When you do it, be sure to do it reverently, even if you are in the middle of a busy airport, on a bus, in your office or at home. You don't have to be serious, but be reverent.

Right now, for example, I am sitting on the balcony of my hotel room in Jamaica. It is 80 degrees. It is 10 below zero in Minnesota. The air is warm and soothing. Night has just fallen. The harbor lights twinkle playfully. The lights on the surrounding hills outline the shape of the town, like the lights on a Christmas tree. The lilting, soothing sound of the waves on the shore takes me away for a moment. I come back and am aware that Linda and the kids are inside our rooms. I think of them and feel warm, connected and grateful. I notice how relaxed my body is. I feel joy. I feel whole. Every muscle in my body feels relaxed. The soles of my feet feel relaxed and warm. My calves feel relaxed and warm. My legs, stomach, back, shoulders, neck, arms, forehead and hands feel relaxed and warm. Images start to flood my consciousness. I remember what it used to be like when I was never relaxed. I remember how I used to have to ingest chemicals to make myself feel this way. I feel grateful for my recovery. I feel proud of myself for working so hard to get healthier. I thank my Higher Power for all that I now have, especially in light of what little I had a few short years ago. I reflect upon how my life and that of Linda and the kids would be different had we simply been born in another country; how our struggles would be different; how our opportunities would be different. I know that when I awaken tomorrow, I will again see a Third World country. I feel some guilt and some sadness. I know that I can't cure world hunger by myself. I try to center myself again and know that I can only do what I am able.

Can you see and feel what I am doing here? I pay attention to what is outside of me. I pay attention to my body. I pay attention to my heart and soul and mind. This is a big part of what I mean by noticing and listening. Be sure to notice the small, seemingly insignificant stuff, which I believe is the most valuable and important in life.

As Chungliang Al Huang put it, "We thus become addicts of the *peak* experiences and devalue the virtues of the ordinary. . . . See the beauty in the faded bloom . . . Let yourself remember the small wonders of this earth . . . For a moment you may find yourself tuned into the beat of the cosmic dance that goes on even when the colored spotlights are out."

If you have trouble thinking of some of the "little things" in life that are wonderful, get a copy of Barbara Ann Kipfer's *14,000 Things To Be Happy About.*

Put It Into Daily Practice.

Being quiet and letting in your environment can be done very formally and deliberately. If you're stuck or confused with an issue you can set aside some time, go somewhere special and be still. But once this kind of heightened awareness becomes a habit, you can call on it whenever you need it. It can be especially powerful if you need to identify your feelings, even in the heat of an argument.

Watch how Bob and Sue use their noticing skills to help themselves be clearer in the midst of a discussion:

Bob and Sue have been discussing their sexual relationship. They are both being careful not to hurt the other's feelings. They care a lot about each other. They know that sexuality can be a delicate subject.
Sue: So, what are you trying to say, Bob?

Bob: Uh, I, uh . . . I'm not sure. I mean, I love how we make love. It's just that . . .

Sue: It's just that what? You're beating around the bush so much, you're scaring me! Is there something awful you need to tell me? (Sue is expressing her fear, and there is also some anger in her voice because she needs Bob to answer directly so that her fear of the unknown will stop.)

Bob: (The testiness in Sue's voice has jarred him. Instead of escalating the anger, which is how he might have handled it in the past, Bob takes a deep breath and in a split-second goes inside of himself, images what he feels, notices that Sue is both afraid and angry, notices that he would feel the same way if she were being vague with him, notices that her anger has triggered his fear and his anger and then uses his anger not to retaliate and escalate, but to move past his fear to respond truthfully, tenderly and with empathy.) No, Sue. It's nothing awful. And it's nothing about you. I just wanted to ask you if you like to look at my body. You know, if it turns you on to see me naked. I've never asked a woman that and it's scary to ask. It seems so . . . so silly . . . I feel so vulnerable asking you that. Kind of self-centered or something.

Sue: (Breathes a sigh of relief, smiles warmly, not at all in condescension, and notices her fear and anger evaporate into thin air.) Oh, Bob, that's one of the things that I love so much about you. Your willingness to show me that vulnerable side. And absolutely, positively, yes! I find you wildly sexy and attractive and I love to look at your body!

Bob: (His fear and anger evaporate into thin air, too. He smiles warmly back at her.) Thanks. I'm glad you feel that way. It feels good to be sexy and attractive to you. I like that.

Sue: How about you?

Bob: Me?

Sue: Sure. Do you like to look at me?

Bob: Oh, yes! I find you wildly sexy and attractive, too!

Sue: That feels good to me, too. I like that.

What could have been a very angry, hurtful interchange turned into a beautiful, simple intimacy between two people who were both strong and vulnerable at the same time. Interchanges like these form the real core of intimacy. As you re-read the above dialogue, be sure to notice and listen so that you can see how much really happened that can't be expressed in mere words.

TWO EXAMPLES

Losing Your Temper

Let's imagine that you've had a particularly long day at work. You're tired. You've been under a lot of pressure all day. Your boss came down pretty hard on you at 3:30, there was an accident on the freeway and it took you an extra hour to get home. You finally pull into the driveway at 6:30, exhausted and frazzled. You walk into the house hoping to find some respite from the cold cruel world outside. You hang up your coat in the closet, go upstairs to change into some comfortable clothes, and on the way to your bedroom you trip over your wife's briefcase that she left in the hallway because she was late for a 5:00 p.m. meeting with a friend. As you hit the floor and twist your ankle, you hear the front door open and your wife cheerily yells up the stairs, "Honey! I'm home! Do you want to go out for dinner?"

It all happens so fast that you don't have time to process it. You react impulsively, out of fatigue and frustration, yelling back at her, "Damn! Damn you! I just tripped over your stupid briefcase and all you can say is 'Honey!' How dare you? Can't you *ever* think about anybody but yourself? I'm so sick and tired of falling over your junk all the time. You're such a slob! You've *always* been a slob! Damn you, anyway!" You lie on the floor as she rushes upstairs to see what's the matter. Her face is riddled with hurt, fear and anger. Guilt rushes in as you begin to attempt an apology. But the damage is already done. She rushes into the bedroom, slams and locks the door and yells back at you, "I didn't deserve that!" You lie there for a few moments, emotionally confused, wounded. Then you go downstairs and fix something for dinner, hoping that it will blow over soon.

That's the scenario. In terms of noticing and listening, it's what comes next that's really important. When our emotions get out of control like this, we feel guilty and ashamed. Then we feel scared that the person we have hurt will go away from us. If these feelings get too big too fast, we will then over-react in the opposite direction to make up for it. After this kind of scenario, many men try to make it better by extreme means.

I might rush out and buy my wife that expensive leather coat she's wanted, even though I know that the cost of the coat will put us back severely. This will put even more stress on both of us, setting us up for more angry outbursts later on. In truth, she doesn't want the coat as a peace offering, and she is just as worried about the finances as I am. But she accepts it nervously, uncomfortably, because she feels badly for me. Because she knows that she does leave things lying around the house in dangerous places. The two of us collude in this maladaptive solution to our discomfort. In Figure 13.1 I have drawn the sequence of events here as just described.

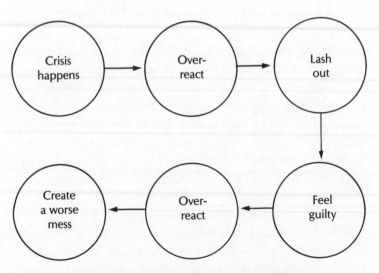

Figure 13.1. Not Noticing And Listening

The problem with this sequence is that nothing gets resolved. No one ever has to be accountable for what they did to contribute to the problem. She doesn't have to own up to her dangerous messiness, and I don't have to own up to my outbursts of rage. Therefore, the system is ready and waiting for the next outburst, which is crouched and ready to pounce the next time either of us is under too much stress.

Now let's look at the same event, but with two people who have begun to practice noticing and listening. We'll begin at what looks like the end of it all. I have tripped and fallen, my wife yells upstairs, I yell at her, she locks herself in the bedroom, and I find myself lying on the floor in a heap of emotional confusion. I pick myself up, walk downstairs and lick my emotional wounds.

Then, I notice and listen. I look back over my day. It got out of control. I didn't give myself enough lead time to account for possible traffic tieups on the freeway. I could have talked to a friend about my bruised ego before I left work. I was going to, but I was too ashamed after the boss' tongue-lashing. I read back through my memory banks. This has happened before! Okay, I say. What else? She shouldn't leave her stuff lying around, but I've lived with her for 25 years. This wasn't really the issue. My ego-strength was low. I was tired. I'm not an evil person. She's not an evil person. It was a bad day *for me*. She was in a cheery mood. Now we're both bummed out. Hmmmmm. I stand in the kitchen, reflecting on what happened. I start to cool down. The issues come into focus inside of my mind. Neither of us is bad. I was in a bad mood. She left her stuff out. I said something hurtful to her. It wasn't constructive. Is all lost? No. We love each other. We know how to communicate. I need to own up to *my part* before anything else will happen.

Now I have something to go on. I wait a while to be sure that I'm clear. I walk upstairs, scared but hopeful. I knock on the door and state directly, "I'm sorry that I yelled at you. I didn't handle that right." I don't make excuses. I don't beg. I come from a position of humility and strength. I stand there in silence for a minute, waiting. The door opens. We look each other in the eyes. She feels understood. Her feelings were hurt. She apologizes for leaving her briefcase in the darkened hallway. The abyss between us begins to dissolve. She laughs about how she thought I had broken my leg or worse when she rushed up the stairs. I laugh about thinking that she intentionally laid a trap for me because she knew I had had a bad day. The abyss is gone. We hug, and then kiss affectionately. We go out to dinner. Over dinner, both relaxed now, I ask if she would at least make an effort to put things to the side of the hallway next time so that I won't wind up in the hospital. Days later I notice she has made an effort. She notices that I'm not losing my temper much either. I thank her for her efforts. She thanks me for mine. I make a concerted effort to see "tough days" as hot-spots. I see that when I am tired or ego-bruised, I need to make extra efforts to care for myself and for our relationship. Life seems just a little bit smoother these days. I seem to have a better handle on my reactions. I like this Noticing and Listening stuff.

In Figure 13.2, I have drawn the sequence of events as they happened when I noticed and listened to my environments.

Who's Safe?

Before I was able to admit my fear, I used to love to be around scary people. I was drawn to unrecovering addicts and offenders like a moth is attracted to a flame. The excitement and unpredictability gave me a big adrenalin rush. There was always fun in the air. Anything could happen. And often anything did. Before I had some good recovery under my belt, I liked to hang around business associates who promised me I'd become a millionaire if only I'd stick with them a little longer. So I'd stick with them a little longer and end up broke. I got into destructive relationships with women where there was always great promise of affection and emotional excitement, only to discover that there was nothing there at all except loneliness and misery.

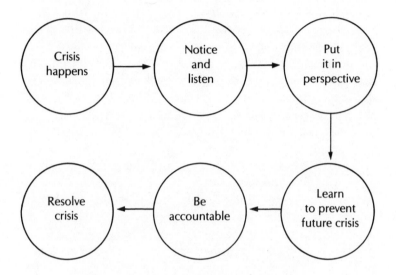

Figure 13.2. Noticing And Listening

Then I started to notice the consequences of ignoring my fear. I made a long list of the consequences. I noticed that when I ignored my healthy fear, I let scary people use me. I got into emotional messes with people that were very hard to get out of. I turned my fear into anger and then punished people with it. I noticed that I didn't trust anyone because the people I chose to be with weren't trustworthy. Plenty of trustworthy people were out there, but I didn't choose to hang around with them because they weren't exciting! So I came to believe that no one was trustworthy.

At last, I owned up to my part in all of this. I noticed that I could choose to stay away from scary people, but that I would have to be alone now and then as a result. I chose to be alone now and then. I waited, noticed and listened. I listened inside of myself. I noticed who was safe and who wasn't. Then I started to find people who were safe. I found more and more of them. I began to cherish those relationships and I began to value them.

When I met Linda, I didn't quite know what to do. She was honest, clear, honorable, willing to take healthy risks and affectionate. She had boundaries, values and integrity. We fell in love. We were scared. We talked. We shared. We learned to fight fair. We valued each other's safety. We didn't put up with abuse from each other. We took risks in the relationship And now we have a marriage that just gets better and better, warmer and deeper with every passing year.

Linda is by no means boring, and she certainly isn't a pushover. She and I feel safe with each other, an absolute necessity in a good relationship. It was worth all of that practice at noticing and listening to my fear to find such a wonderful person. We never would have been able to put this relationship together or nurture it for years if we had not also learned to notice and listen to ourselves. The nice thing about having this skill is that it adds to our lives every day. Because every day we are able to share something new with each other — some new feeling, insight, memory, observation, hope, dream, fantasy or feeling.

Learn to notice and listen. It's worth it.

14

Be A
Man Of
Integrity
And Honor

n a previous chapter, we looked at some possible heroes and male role models. As you consider the men you admire, I encourage you to consider how you can become a hero in your own neighborhood, because looking up to other men won't help us unless we put into practice some of the things we've learned from them. As I look back at the men on my list, I am struck by one common thread. Each in his own way seems to possess integrity and honor that is notable and rare. As I ponder those two words, I am reminded that they have taken quite a beating since my early teens, 30 years ago.

TARNISHED INTEGRITY

Integrity and Honor

I am neither a historian nor good at remembering details, but I can sit here and list in my mind scores of examples of how integrity and honor have been threatened in the past 30 years. I am struck by the role of televison and mass-communications in exposing the dishonor and infamy that have befallen so many public figures. Many politicians complain that they are under an "unfair microscope" because of the press and instant worldwide communication, but I am not convinced that it is unfair. It is simply the way it is now, and we have to learn to live in the here and now, not in "the good old days." I believe that we will always have the right to expect our leaders to be honorable, as defined by the times and the culture in which we are currently living. This is why the Constitution of the United States was designed to be changed when enough of us deemed it appropriate to do so. Please keep that in mind as you think about your heroes and role models.

John F. Kennedy

John F. Kennedy, adored by millions around the world, is said to have been the first American politician to understand and effectively use the media to his powerful advantage. As a nation we were entranced by what we saw on television — a handsome young family loved by all; brothers who were charming, caring, but tough when the chips were down; a bride and two young children right out of a storybook. It was only years later that America was slowly exposed to some of the painful and frightening truths beneath the fantasy image of Camelot.

I have spoken with many Americans who would vote for JFK in an instant if he were alive today, despite all of the uncomfortable truths that have been revealed. My gut tells me they say that because they're still in that trance, and that were JFK to enter politics today with his apparently severe untreated sexual addiction, he wouldn't have a chance at getting elected president. But then in today's climate of recovery, perhaps his addiction would have been treated by the time he was ready to run for president. Who knows?

One of the most notable and symptomatic sayings to come out of the Kennedy Empire was, "Kennedys don't cry," which, as Claudia Black pointed out years ago, is one of the hallmarks of an alcoholic/addictive system: Don't Talk, Don't Trust, Don't Feel. Perhaps someone in the Kennedy family would have gone to an Adult Children of Alcoholics meeting and got into recovery prior to JFK running for president today.

In any event, America has taken it on the chin when it comes to integrity and honor. We saw our beloved leaders gunned down in their prime, and in JFK's case, one of the serious theories about his assassination was that he was killed by his own government. We got ourselves into a war that seemed to have no honor to begin with, and then we slapped in the face the very soldiers we sent to fight in that war. If they objected to fighting, we threw them in jail. If they fought, we treated them like nonpeople when they returned home. What a horrible, awful, crazy, double-bind!

Richard Nixon

In the '70s we saw an American president get caught in his own lies and domestic political miscalculations so that he had to resign his presidency. Richard Nixon did a "damned fine job" with foreign policy but he sure fouled up at home. In all fairness to him, other presidents have engaged in hardball politics and nasty campaigns. He just did it so blatantly and ineptly that it wound up demoralizing a whole nation. Nixon was definitely not covered with Teflon as was his descendant, Ronald Reagan. Nixon's continued denials leave a bad taste in our mouths even today, which is sad. I find people to be quite forgiving once a fellow man owns up, admits to his mistakes and then tries to make amends. To amend as a way of avoiding admission of wrongdoing doesn't set well in our unconscious minds.

The Me-First Eighties

The Watergate tragedy was followed in the '80s by a generation of people who seemed to care little for each other. Our heroes were defined by how much they could acquire. The price of "honor" was one Mercedes in the garage. "Integrity" cost a Mercedes, a $1,000 suit and a Rolex watch. While we *talked* about the evils of Communism, drug cartels and world poverty, the gap between the rich and the poor in America widened so dramatically that today we are again on the brink of social disaster.

Our political, business and religious leaders did not fare well in the '80s, either. Kennedy imitator Senator Gary Hart wound up on the political cutting room floor because of his escapades with Donna Rice, as well as his arrogant misjudgment of the American public and the power of instant media exposure. Ronald Reagan became embroiled in "Irangate" but managed to escape unscathed, some would say, because he was "likeable" and "believable." If Richard Nixon had done Irangate, he would have been crucified for it. Then there were The Keating Five—Democrats Cranston, DeConcini, Riegle, Glenn and Republican McCain—who have been investigated for their involvement in the Savings And Loan Crisis. It is estimated that the government's seizure of Keating's S&L will cost us, the U.S. taxpayers, up to $2 billion. This is not good.

Jim Bakker and Jimmy Swaggart showed that many televangelists are just unrecovering sexual addicts and slick salesmen who do a great job of fooling the naive in America. More and more cases of sexual exploitation of children by religious figures are coming to trial every year. It seems I can't travel to a city in America that doesn't have a priest or minister on trial for sexual abuse of kids.

Ivan Boesky earned himself a jail sentence for his Wall Street crimes. Leona Helmsley was caught evading taxes in almost humorously petty ways, and it turned out that she was pretty darned ruthless and uncaring in some not-so-humorous ways. Even Donald Trump, whom everyone secretly admired for his guts and glamour, fell from grace via his tacky love affair with Marla Maples, which coincided with his drifting back down to earth to join the ranks of mere millionaires.

I can feel it across the nation. Everywhere I go, people are wondering if "honor" is a word with so little meaning that it won't be in the next edition of Webster's Dictionary. In some cases the lack of honor is simply terrifying. One of the strengths of men, supposedly, is our sense of fair play, which confuses me when I look at the shocking rape statistics in this country. Colleges and universities around the U.S. know how bad it is because their male students seem to be on a raping binge.

When I first saw examples of the brutal, calloused way in which rapes are happening on college campuses in a national news special, I wondered what planet I was on. Some fraternities actually have special code words for their form of gang-rape during which a female student is singled out, encouraged to become intoxicated and then videotaped as all of the guys rape her. In one gruesome case reported in *People* magazine, the 19-year-old freshman girl was raped in her date's fraternity house bedroom and then taken to a shower room where at least two others raped her and brutalized her. The authors of the article noted that the rapist's sentence of one year minus a day was severe for a date-rape case, and therefore, a victory.

But the real victory will emerge when fathers and mothers raise sons and daughters who respect themselves, respect each other and have a strong internal sense of integrity. The kind of brotherhood displayed in these groups of men is not one I would choose to be a part of. A man of honor would never do something like this to a woman. We need to raise men of integrity in America, not violent, dishonorable men.

The problem of rape is certainly not confined to college campuses, but somehow we expect more from "nice middle-class kids." Unfortunately, nice middle-class kids are hurting, too. The same is true when we look at ethnic and racial hatred on and off college campuses.

Dartmouth University, long a bastion of liberal humanism in this country, has been embroiled in racial and ethnic clashes for the past couple of years. Intolerance, racial killings, beatings, hate groups, the Ku Klux Klan. They're on the rise in America.

The brutal beating of Rodney King by a group of Los Angeles policemen in March of 1991, shown repeatedly on national television, means that something is very wrong with us. It's frightening to think that we have to keep reverting back to our instinctual, animal rage every time we have a few problems in this country. The economy is bad? Let's hate someone. We can't control our own credit card spending? Hey, let's put a few semi-automatic weapons in the hall closet, just in case. Can't make enough money the "good old-fashioned way"? Well, why not lie, cheat, and steal? If your collar and your skin are both white, no one will care, will they?

CULTIVATING INTEGRITY IN OUR CHILDREN

After all, honor is just for show, isn't it? Aren't we a media society? Isn't it what's on the outside that makes the man? Does it matter what we do behind closed doors as long as we are able to keep our public image from being tarnished? George Washington did what he did for raw power, right? Actually not. George Washington could have been King of America but he turned it down to retire to his farm. George III of England predicted that if Washington were able to do that, he would "be the greatest man in the world." Washington was also "the only founder of this nation who managed to free his slaves" (Chalberg, 1984).

We *do* have healthy heroes in America, but no one will notice unless our mothers and fathers become healthy heroes first. Boys from healthy families don't gang-rape women. These dysfunctional families may look like healthy families on the outside because our definitions of health have become so superficial — money, things, raw power — but they aren't. It would be impossible for a healthy boy or man to rape someone. Impossible.

How do boys learn to have integrity and honor? We learn it from parents who have it. As you might expect, we don't learn it from parents who *talk* about it. We learn from parents who *act* with integrity and honor. That is why in our first two books, Linda and I stressed the importance of parents healing their own psychological wounds before trying to "save" their children. You can lecture and pontificate about values, morality and honorable behavior, but if you aren't acting that way, your kids will somehow know it and begin acting out your fraud for you. They will become like you. It's pretty straightforward.

Young adults who have clear values, self-respect and good self-esteem come from families where Dad and Mom had clear values, self-respect and good self-esteem. When children see parents living their values, children learn to live those values. Where we get confused is in how we define that. Among other things, I want my children to respect themselves, to stick up for themselves, to respect others, to value human life, to be spiritual and to care passionately about something. That's a pretty tall order and I know that as imperfect human beings, the order is never completely filled.

More importantly, I know that the way in which they fill the order may be very different than mine. I know they may choose a different church to go to or no church at all. This does not negate their spirituality. I know they may choose a career over marriage and family or choose family over career. I know that they may be Republicans or Democrats; it doesn't matter. But I do want them to have a reason for it and to be committed to the things they say they are committed.

In other words, my children are separate from me, but they have a right to learn some good things from me as they grow up. Children whose parents talk a good story but don't practice it in their own lives grow up to have secret contempt for their parents. They also grow up very confused and very shallow themselves, and find it difficult to be committed to a set of values that is their own. In other words, fraudulent parents produce children who feel like frauds and who therefore don't respect themselves.

For example, many parents talk about "being religious" and go to religious services every week. They preach "at" their children. They say grace at every meal. They pray openly. Then they turn around and live their lives in hatred and fear the rest of the time. In the name of their god, they foist their subtle prejudices on their neighbor who has an ethnic name or a different skin color. In the name of god, they shame their children, control their children abusively and suppress their children's spirituality. They lie to their spouses and friends in private and look great in public. Then when their children grow up and are estranged from them, they cry in outrage at the unfairness of life and at the selfishness of their children.

The bottom line is that if you want to have children of integrity and honor, you must treat yourself, them and others with integrity and honor. You don't have to shove your beliefs down their throats. You don't have to wring your hands night after night wondering if they will turn out okay. You don't have to make them read anything or memorize anything. If you demonstrate integrity and honor on a daily basis, they will grow up to have integrity and honor. It's just that simple. If you want your children to have healthy humility without a lot of unhealthy shame, then work on your own humility, not theirs.

Think about people like Jesus Christ, Mohandas Gandhi, Mother Teresa, Andrei Sakharov, Nelson Mandela, Martin Luther King, Jr., George Washington, Abraham Lincoln — whoever you look up to. Some of them preached, some of them wrote, some did both. But do you know what has been burned into our memories by all of these wonderful people whether or not we have read or heard all that they have said? What we remember is how they lived their lives. *What we find so awe-inspiring is that they actually lived what they preached.*

WHAT IS INTEGRITY?

When I hear the word "integrity" I think of wholeness, honesty, consistency, honor, trust, values, fairness and ethics. I think of the many contemporary men who have been good role models for us in the past 30 years. I think of Jimmy Carter, a man whose tedious leadership style got him so bogged down in the presidency that he couldn't be re-elected, but whose life now is an example of values and honor. Like George Washington who returned to his farm rather than being pronounced king by an adoring America, Carter has returned to the earth, working with his hands to build houses for and with the poor. The values that he proclaimed around the world as President weren't just empty rhetoric as some critics may have thought. He's *still* living those values today, even though it won't help his career one bit.

I think of Elliot Richardson, Attorney General under Richard Nixon, who made the earth-shattering and politically unheard-of-decision to resign rather than fire Special Prosecutor Archibald Cox, as he had been ordered to do by the Nixon Administration. With so many years passed, it would be easy to say, "Well, of course he resigned. Wouldn't anybody have done the same?" But the fact is that very few people have ever shown that kind of moral courage under such intense public scrutiny. The Watergate scandal was still a mass of confusion. Nobody really knew the truth. As far as Richardson knew, he was committing political suicide when he resigned. But he did it anyway.

Integrity is a very difficult thing to maintain. It can hurt a lot at times to have integrity. Honorable leadership isn't easy. Sometimes a man of integrity must make very lonely decisions that open him up to public ridicule, censure or even death. Jesus Christ knew that. Martin Luther King, Jr. knew that. Even South Africa's President F. W. deKlerk knows that. Having morals and "doing the right thing" don't always pay off in the short run. In the long run I believe they do, but certainly not in the short run.

I am saddened when I see our leaders and public figures try to take the quick, easy way to success.

During our 1990 elections here in Minnesota we had a candidate, Jon Grunseth, who was ultimately forced out of the race because of his sexual behavior. Two women came forward and accused him of sexual abuse at a pool party at his house when they were 13 years old. The women who accused Grunseth said that they had been friends of his daughter. There had been an all-day party, the "men" had encouraged the girls to swim nude, they didn't want to. Gruseth had blocked one of them and pulled at her strap, the girls felt dirty and ashamed and scared, and it was long forgotten — until they became women and saw that he was going to become governor. Grunseth denied the accusations despite supporting stories from others. Just before the elections, a woman who claimed to be his mistress came forward and spoke of her affair with Grunseth and said something to the effect that the public Jon Grunseth who was moral, proper and conservative was nothing like the private Jon Grunseth. He dropped out of the race, and as far as I know, still blames his opponents for what happened. In her thoughtful analysis of this sad story written for the *Minneapolis/ St. Paul Magazine*, Lynda McDonnell wrote, "How a man treats his wife, girlfriend, daughters, co-workers and girls down the block is not just a private matter. It should matter to us all."

People make mistakes. We are human beings. We are allowed to make mistakes in our lives. But we are also expected to grow and deepen as human beings as we mature and grow older. A large part of this growing and deepening requires that we hold ourselves accountable for those mistakes, and that we "make amends for them whenever possible."

These aren't just "lofty" principles from the 12 Steps of Alcoholics Anonymous. These are basic principles of living to which everyone should aspire, alcoholic or not. When we are let down, sexually abused, shamed, screamed at, hit or otherwise hurt by another human being, it produces some damage. If it happens with intensity and frequency, we are damaged a lot. But experts in the field of abuse know that the worst damage comes from the betrayal of our own self and truth when (1) the offender who hurt us then denies that anything happened or (2) the offender admits that it happened but denies that it hurt us. Then we really feel crazy on top of the hurt. On the other hand, when a human being makes a mistake, then admits it and stops the abusive behavior, then he is setting us free to heal and get on with our lives, and he is giving us and the world a very powerful example to which we can all aspire.

Another Minnesota Republican, Senator David Durenberger, made some pretty big financial mistakes for which he was censured by Congress. He had been under a lot of personal stress in his life and he did what a lot of public figures had done in the past — he wrote a book and then used it more or less to "launder" campaign contributions. There is no way that this is okay and his colleagues let him know it in no uncertain terms. What happened to him may wind up destroying his political career. But do you know what? Mr. Durenberger redeemed himself as far as I'm concerned. He got up in front of the television cameras and the entire nation and without equivocation he admitted his wrongdoing, he apologized to all of us in Minnesota, he apologized to all of his friends and colleagues in the Senate and he took his punishments like a man.

Linda, who has an uncanny sense about people, turned to me after we watched Durenberger's apology and said, "I believe him. I think this is the worst we'll ever see in him, too." I agreed with her. Some people learn from their mistakes and gain integrity. Others refuse to learn, and they just get more slimey by the day. It feels as if David Durenberger was one of the ones who chose to learn. If so, then he has done more for the State of Minnesota than many will ever realize.

Will we ever know if the tears of regret shed by Jimmy Swaggart and Jim and Tammy Bakker were real, or just manipulations? Will we ever know what happened at Chappaquiddick that night when Ted Kennedy and Mary Jo

Kopechne plunged into the water? Will we ever fully know of Richard Nixon's role in Watergate? Will we ever know the extent of Gary Hart's relationship with Donna Rice? Will we ever know what Jon Grunseth's private life was like? Will we ever know who authorized the assassination of John Kennedy? Probably not. And as a result, there will always be a nagging wound, a mild, low-grade infection, a bit of our own truth that feels just a touch "off." We will go on. We will endure. But there will be a flaw in our sense of wholeness. Something will feel unfinished.

I've said it before in this book, but I'll say it again. Our human capacity for forgiveness is almost limitless if we are given the chance to forgive. It saddens me deeply to see some of our leaders so paralyzed by their own shame and fear that they refuse to give us the chance to forgive. To forgive a past abuse or lie that has been admitted and stopped is divine. To forgive an abuse or deception that is still going on is a form of self-hurt, self-damage and self-deception. We will feel crazy doing it, and we will act crazy around it. That, I believe, is why those two women came forward just before our Minnesota elections in 1990. They were tired of feeling crazy.

WHAT IS A MAN OF INTEGRITY?

There are any number of examples and definitions of integrity, but some key words make up the concept for me:

1. *Trust.* A man of integrity can be trusted. Within reason, he will do what he says he will do. I may not be able to join you for a movie on Friday after I said I would because I might be tired. But if I borrow $100.00 from you today and promise to pay it back next week, I can guarantee that I will pay you back next week unless I have died, gone absolutely totally bankrupt or have been kidnapped.

2. *Values.* A man of integrity has clear values which include an individual's right to life, right to property and the right to his own reality (as long as that reality isn't hurting others). He is willing to take a

stand for those values and proclaim them even when they are unpopular. He doesn't just talk about values, but he lives them.

3. *Respect.* A man of integrity has respect for his own and others' values and beliefs. He respects men, women and children. He respects the environment and he respects the truth.

4. *Fairness.* A man of integrity values fairness. To win for the sake of winning isn't always fair. To overpower a weaker opponent just for the sake of gaining more power or influence isn't fair. To force oneself on another by use of physical force isn't fair, except to defend oneself. To bully others isn't fair. To manipulate others into doing what we want them to do isn't fair. A good, clean, honest fight is fair. Playing by the rules of life as well as the rules of baseball or football is fair. Dishonorable men always break the rules of life. Men of integrity don't.

5. *Consistency.* A man of integrity will be consistent without being rigid or inflexible. This is not a contradiction. Linda can rely on me to be there for her when she really needs my support, and I can rely on her that way, too. When I say that I'll pick up David after school, I will unless I tell her otherwise. We expect each other to follow through with what we promise, and the fact that we follow through gives each of us a sense of consistency and reliability. Let your actions flow from your values and beliefs. If you say you don't believe in taking advantage of others, then don't do it, no matter who is egging you on. That "others do it" isn't a good enough reason to break your own moral principles.

6. *Wholeness.* A man of integrity feels whole and complete inside, not fragmented and broken. Wholeness does not mean that we can't change and grow. I can be whole and still have things to learn about myself. But I have a sense of who I am, where I have been and where I am going with my life.

7. *Tough Decisions.* Perhaps most important of all in terms of living a life of integrity, we as men must be willing and able to make tough, painful decisions. "It is more valuable to be alone than to hurt another person," is a phrase I have said to myself for years. It is also more valuable to be alone than to let others hurt us. It is more valuable to be embarrassed by admission of your mistakes than to leave other people feeling crazy by your denials. It is more valuable to leave a friendship or marriage than to sit by and participate in your loved one's death from alcoholism or other addictive disease. Tough decisions are laced with fear, sadness and regret, but those are each noble human emotions.

I challenge myself every day to try to live by values that let me feel whole, consistent and honorable. I see men around me every day who are living with honor and dignity. Regardless of how many dishonorable men you see around you, remember that there are many more honorable ones. They may not always make the front page of the newspaper, but they're there. Remember, too, that it is never too late to become honorable, to have integrity and to become whole. I challenge you to . . .

Be a man of integrity and honor.

In Search Of A True Human Being

ack in the mid-70s I began to develop a love of movies. I wasn't really sure why at the time. During that time I began to try to write more than just technical articles for psychology journals, and I remember becoming entranced by acting, directing, cinematography, stories, metaphors and other aspects of movie-making and writing in general. Then I remembered that one of the things my father frequently did with us was to take us to the movies. We were especially excited when on a Saturday afternoon, we would drive across the Golden Gate Bridge into San Francisco to see a newly released film at the grand old Cinemascope theater "in the big city." So this rekindling of my love of films means a lot to me now.

It has been especially wonderful to see another film come out recently that touches so many men in so many different ways — the kind of film that everyone from the harshest critics to the guy in the street can admire and relate to. At the time of this writing, I can only assume that *Dances With Wolves* will be nominated for many Academy Awards, and that it will win at least a few.

Dances With Wolves, based on the novel (1988) and screenplay by Michael Blake, and directed by and starring Kevin Costner, managed to reach into the darker soul of America and touch us so gently and respectfully that we were able to feel our national shame, our sadness at the loss of what was and our awe and wonder at the sometimes overwhelming beauty of human beings all at the same time. As usually happens with works of art, many of us were able to feel our own personal sadness, shame, joy and wonder as a result of watching Costner's film.

If you have not already seen this film, I urge you to do so. All of the men with whom I have discussed this film were profoundly touched by it. It is almost as if we walk into the theater blindfolded by a long piece of surgical gauze wrapped around and around our heads, and as we sit and watch *Dances With Wolves*, we let Blake and Costner gently remove layer after layer of the bandage until we have seen and smelled and touched and tasted the lost soul of America and the pain and beauty inside ourselves. I will be very surprised if this film does not become a timeless classic.

If you see have seen this film, go see it again. Then I urge you to share your feelings with someone afterwards. Not your opinions about the film but rather, the feelings that stirred inside you while watching the film! These are two very different assignments.

INTEGRITY

This film is about integrity. It is a story of a man's discovery of himself. It is a story of the shameful, sad, addictive, greedy, dishonest side of America. The story captures the beauty of the Lakota Nation, showing with subtlety and grace the harmony and wisdom of their relationship among themselves and with nature. I still shudder when I peek from behind my gauze bandages to see what my Caucasian brothers and sisters did to an entire nation of people. I feel sick when I realize that we did it in the name of God, which is what the principle of Manifest Destiny was really about.

The film is filled with obvious heroes, and then there is the heroic Kevin Costner himself, who took a huge risk and turned down chances for leading roles in several important films so that he could pursue his own dream of making this movie (Rosen & Johnson, 1990). It is filled with subtle heroes, too.

When I walked out of the movie theater after viewing *Dances With Wolves,* I realized that it has been my great fortune to have found many heroes around me over the years — they are the courageous men with whom I have worked in men's groups and from whom I have learned so much for long. They are common men like you and me, rather than stars or national leaders. Many of them were perched on the brink of death because of their addictiveness, their depression or their suicidal and hopeless feelings, and who then chose life over death. As one man in group put it, "We chose to walk with those who are awake rather than to continue to walk with those who are asleep."

I appreciate that metaphor. It describes what each man must choose if he is to become whole. It is what integrity is all about. It requires tremendous risk with no guarantees. It demands respect of self and respect of humanity. It demands personal honesty, and honesty with others. It requires letting go. And it simply cannot happen without spirituality. *Dances With Wolves* is a romantic and spiritual film, and the changes that I see men making in their lives are truly spiritual changes, as well as heroic ones.

INSIDE A MAN'S HEART

I began to ask the guys in my groups what stood out the most for them in this film — what touched them the most. And each man said something different, as if the film were a peephole into the farthest reaches of their hearts. Each man was touched by different symbols or events in the film, but there were common threads. Many men spoke warmly of the nonverbal communication between the men in the film, and of the natural beauty of the Native American practice of men sitting around the fire and talking. "Actually talking together!" one group member exclaimed. I looked around the room with the nine of us sitting in a circle — talking and laughing and crying and working out our differences together — and I smiled warmly inside.

What do men want? What is inside the heart of a man? What I have found is that as each man takes the herculean risk to walk into his own personal wilderness, and as each man then takes the risk to get out and meet the neighbors he thinks are his enemies, he discovers that there are some universal wounds inside of his heart. If he goes deep enough, he will find that they are the same wounds that women experience, too — fear of loneliness and destruction, insufficient love and nurturing, shame, guilt and feelings of emptiness. And as men continue to look inside of themselves and find those wounds and then let other men gently touch the wounds, they find that the wounds begin to heal. Robert Bly (1990) writes of "Father-Hunger." This says it well. We are starved for guidance, for friendship, for brotherhood.

What do men want?

The hundreds of men with whom I have worked want to be true human beings. They want . . .

To Feel

They are tired of being stuck inside their heads all the time. They don't want to give up logic but they want to be able to fill in that feeling side a little better. They want to be able to grieve when it's appropriate so they don't have to carry around pain piled on top of pain for the rest of their lives. They want to honor their fear so they are not foolish and self-destructive any longer. They want to respect their hurt so they can heal.

To Befriend

They are tired of being lonely — of having no true friends — but they never learned how to "do friendship" because no one ever taught them. They are hungry for what Herb Goldberg called "the Lost Art of Buddyship" (*The Harzards of Being Male*, 1976). They want to be able to feel close without having to create false closeness in a bar and through the bottom of a beer bottle or a martini glass. They don't necessarily want to give up watching football, but they know that there's more to friendship than sports.

To Love

Most of them want a primary romantic relationship in their lives — with a woman if they're straight, with a man if they're gay — but they don't know how to do that without being addicted, an offender or being a victim. They struggle with painful power imbalances in their primary relationships. They want to love and be loved but they haven't had everyday heroes in their childhoods from whom to learn how to love and be loved without making a mess of it.

To Work

They all want work that is meaningful and that they can be proud of. They don't want to give up being providers, but they just want to provide in ways that fill them up instead of emptying them all the time.

To Father

Those with children want to be good fathers. Some of the deepest pain they share is about the hurts they see carried by their children, some of which is caused by them and the family systems from which they came. They want to be mentors, role models and heroes to their children, and they struggle with all of the crazy things about fathering that they learned from their own parents and from society. They struggle with setting limits, being too nice and then being too rigid and authoritarian.

To Be Whole

They want to feel whole inside. They want to have personal integrity where before there was little. They want an identity inside of themselves, taking risks without being reckless. They want to nurture without being enmeshed victims or rescuers. They long for male role models who are honest, true and whole, rather than manipulative, deceitful and fragmented.

To Heal

When they speak of their fathers, so many of these good men feel a deep pain. They can't always articulate it, but I can see it in a lost look or a vacant distant stare. I can feel it in their hunger for a Dad who was there for them, who cared, who did things with them, who guided and taught them. They are hungry for knowledge of how to be strong and male without being weak, aggressive and abusive. It is a longing that caused thousands of men across the country to cry deeply at the end of Kevin Costner's other powerful film, *Field of Dreams*. The new "men's movement" is right about this one — men want to heal their Father Wound.

FINDING A TRUE HUMAN BEING

The men with who I work know these goals are achievable because they have seen other men do it in therapy or elsewhere. And yet it is frustrating as they begin their healing process because their usual goal-directed, analytic approaches don't seem to help, at least not for the intuitive-feeling parts of their work. It is especially frustrating because most of us don't know what it is that we're shooting for in the first place. We don't know what a man is. We know there's a trail, and we have some hunches about where it leads, but we have no one to lead us.

We can learn much from observing others. As we watch how other people and other cultures do things, we can begin to get some ideas of how we want to be. It's what healthy adolescents do all the time. They "try on different hats." They look to their mentors and role models to learn how to be grown-up men. They are affected by movie stars, rock stars and political leaders and sports heroes.

As I process films like *Field of Dreams* and *Dances With Wolves* with clients to see what touched them most about the characters, I am struck by the universality of the responses. In fact, as I compiled a list of traits describing the heroes in these films I am struck by how similar the lists are to the list of Healthy Adult Traits that I presented in Chapter 7. They all seemed to embody the best of what constitutes a real man and a healthy man. I believe that a healthy man and true male human being are one in the same. And I believe that characters like these in films like these can be helpful in giving us something to shoot for in our recoveries from our male bondage as long as we realize that we are not characters in a film, and that we must live our our reality.

So, what's so special about the characters in these films? Did the Lakota Indians have something we didn't? Does Kevin Costner know something we don't? Do we all have to build a ballfield in our backyards? Here is the list of traits describing the men in these two films:

Knowledgeable In The Ways Of Men. These men knew about "guy-things" like baseball, hunting, building and fixing things, farming, how to lead a war-party, make a bow and arrow, set up camp, sit in a circle and make decisions, negotiate, fight, protect and defend, provide, write poetry, protest war, and love with consistency and honor.

Independence And Self-Direction. They were each "their own man," so to speak. They could stand firm with difficult decisions in the face of opposition from the group when necessary. They had self-reliance. They could pursue a dream and endure loneliness and insecurity in that pursuit.

Interdependence. They relied on each other and could work for the common good of all. They allowed themselves to be nurtured and were able to nurture and care for others when appropriate.

Fierceness And Tenderness. Confucius said that "only the truly kind man knows how to love and how to hate." A whole person can be both tender and fierce, when each are appropriate.

Openness And Innocence. Abraham Maslow (1954) noted these traits as being characteristic of self-actualizing people. It is an innocence without being dangerously naive; and a willingness to look at the world with an entirely fresh perspective every now and then. It is that innocence and openness which made the Lakota characters so warm and real, and which has made many of Kevin Costner's film roles so memorable. It is a childlike quality without being childish.

Risk. Adventurousness can come in the form of building a baseball field in one's cornfield, despite the seeming folly of it; or in making friends with a white man who might just as well stab you in the back as look at you. Risk with wisdom is a trait of a healthy man or woman. Sometimes, like John Dunbar, we need to just get on our horse and ride out to meet our new neighbors, even though we might be scared to death to meet them.

Home-Centeredness. In both *Field of Dreams* and *Dances With Wolves* we see exquisite examples of the importance of home, family, companionship, loyalty to family, friendship, togetherness, and family solidarity. In the latter film, we see John Dunbar struggle internally with just exactly where his home is, as he returns to his "soldier fort," then to his lodge with the Lakota and back again, until he realizes where home really is.

Decisiveness. Decision-making is essential to survival and to "being in the world." Action is important. Decisions almost always have an up side and a down side to them. The ability to take wise, thoughtful action is the sign of a healthy society or tribe. Watching the respectful decision-making inside of the Lakota lodge was a lesson in healthy family process. Watching the decisions of the men in both films was a wonder to behold.

Tact. The quiet tact between men is truly one of the joys of working with men in group, and is one of the joys of being a man who has men friends. Men are just as sensitive and caring as women when we are taught and allowed to show that care in masculine ways — when our ways are respected rather than belittled or compared to women's ways.

Gratitude. For many men, this is miserably confused with being weak, defenseless and dangerously vulnerable. But as most of us in 12-Step programs gratefully learn, this gift brings a whole new level of power-healthy power. And it brings peace, balance and joy into life as well. Consider the gratitude expressed by thousands of men to Kevin Costner for his performance in *Field of Dreams,* for the healing that happened as a result of that film. Men without gratitude become tyrants and despots, nazis and fascists.

Humility. Much the same can be said of humility, too. Rather than making a man weak, true humility actually brings us in direct connection with the universe, with ourselves and with our male power. A man who must be God is a dangerous man — an infant in an adult body with adult strength but no wisdom. A humble man can yield when necessary. A humble man can ride into battle one day and fight to protect his home and family; be grateful the next day that he is still alive and pray to his Higher Power for the guidance and strength to be a good man with all those around him. A humble man can admit that there are forces out there over which he has no control, like a tornado, a thundering herd of buffalo and whether or not another person will love him. Humility and power are not opposites.

Humor. In his book, *Why Men Are The Way They Are,* Warren Farrell (1986) writes that one of the traits of men he likes is outrageousness, which I think is actually a

combination of risk-taking, adventurousness and decisiveness, all tempered with a healthy dose of humor. Healthy
humor is life-enhancing and energizing; it helps to diffuse
tension in a positive way. It promotes positive and creative
problem-solving and lets us see both the ridiculous and
the sublime in the universe.

One of John F. Kennedy's favorite sayings, from *The
Ramayana*, was, "There are three things which are real.
God, human folly and laughter. The first two are beyond
our comprehension, so we must do what we can with the
third." I have spoken with very few women who have not
said that a sense of humor in a man is very important and
very appealing. If you get the chance, watch *Field of Dreams*
and *Dances With Wolves* with an eye and an ear for the
humor. I trust that you will see how gentle, how warm,
how appropriate, and how uplifting those moments are
and how much they enrich both films. Good, healthy,
non-sarcastic, non-destructive humor is almost a work of
art, which is probably why women value it so much!

Poetry And Art. Poetry and art? That's right. Strong
guys write poetry, cry at sad movies, appreciate beauty
and value wisdom and truth. The storytellers in so many
cultures were the ones with the wisdom and power. A
man who can write a poem as well as cut down a tree and
build a hut is a man of greater power than a man who can
only cut down a tree. The research on identity development in college students suggests that men who write
creatively and poetically in their journals, rather than just
logging the day's events, are able to find their identities
much sooner.

Spirituality. Many of you who have read the two books
that Linda and I wrote know how we understand spirituality. In keeping with the movies that I have been writing
about here, I would invite you to ponder this: I found
more spirituality in these two films than in a month of
Sundays in some churches.

Spirituality is a relationship with something out there
that is beyond us. It is a willingness to hear and respond
to the distant voices in the universe that call us to unique

and creative action. It is a childlike sense of awe and wonder about the universe. It is the ability to respond to the humanity in each human being we meet. It is the ability to look up at a starry night sky and feel totally insignificant in one moment, and in that very same moment, to feel connected and at one with the universe. It is the ability to let oneself be overwhelmed by the beauty of the prairie, the mountains, the sea, a cornfield, a friendship with a man, or a love relationship with a woman, without being overwhelmed by these things. I'll leave it up to you to figure that one out. Clearly, it is difficult, if not impossible, to be spiritual while we are practicing a major addiction, while we are denying our inner being or our inner feelings and truth, while we are routinely deceiving or abusing others. These things do not permit relationship. And spirituality is relationship. Likewise, spirituality is not possible without a healthy dose of humility or gratitude.

Ethics And Honor. I devoted most of an entire chapter to this one because I felt that it is becoming a lost trait in our culture. I ask you to look around you and notice who in your life is the most honorable. He may not be the most famous, or the richest, because a lot of people have become rich and famous lately by being dishonorable. Notice how it feels safe and respectful to be around a truly honorable person. Notice that you walk away from him feeling clearer and stronger, not slimy and diminished. I am pleased to see many men trying harder to be ethical and honorable. It will save our nation and our planet.

Feelings. It is very important for men to understand that having all of our feelings makes us strong in ways that will not harm us or others. We do not have to express our feelings like women. We need to express our feelings like men. But we need to express all of them when and where it is appropriate. It may not be safe to cry at work, but if we need to cry, we need to find a safe place in which to do it. To only do it in the company of women means that we are stuck. We need to have our anger without raging or being passive-aggressive. We need to have our fear and shame. We need to have all our feelings.

The idea of becoming a true human being does not mean we have to do it perfectly. I hope I have made it clear in this book that above all, we are human. We make mistakes. We hurt. We fall down. We learn from the fall. And we try again. I just think that every ten years or so we need to sit down as a nation and evaluate where we've been, where we're going and who we are. We need to re-establish and reaffirm our values and beliefs. We need to be committed to something. If we don't affirm our values, we'll awaken one day and wish we'd never been born. I think we have a lot going for us as a nation and the men of America have a chance to make that even better. So c'mon guys. Let's get to work.

We can't all produce, direct and star in a beautiful film that is loved by all. But we can do one thing that is very important:

We can all become men.

5

AFTER
ALL
IS SAID
AND
DONE

*The truth is, there's more to life
than movies.*

Kevin Costner

Take Some Little Risks

are to grow up. Have values. Be fair in your dealings with others. Trust yourself. Feel your feelings. Find your dignity. Hope. Care. Respect your body. Love. Be separate. Have fun. *Be A Grown-Up Man.*

As I bring this book to a close, I am reminded of some wisdom that I learned many years ago from St. Paul psychologist Sondra Smalley, one of the first people to write about or treat co-dependency.

In working with people who grew up in traumatic families, Sondra found that we get stuck a lot — we get paralyzed, in a rut, unable to move forwards or backwards. One of the exercises that she had her clients do was to "try anything different" if they were really stuck.

It seemed so simple, yet when I tried it myself or with my own clients, it worked very well. "Anything different" means driving home a different route after work, trying a different flavor ice cream if you always get pistachio or saying "I'd like to choose the movie we see this Sunday" if you always let the other person choose.

I have known for quite some time that the little things in life make it worthwhile. For the first half of my life I lived on the emotional roller coaster of my parents' marriage — extreme highs and lows, lots of intensity and conflict, huge risks followed by huge periods of stagnation and paralyzing fear.

Men and women who are in recovery from addictions know well that this addiction to intensity is dangerous and that it robs us of the true joy that life offers. We also know that the extremes in life are what define serious dysfunction. Taking no risks at all makes us bored, boring and paralyzed. Taking too dangerous risks or too many risks causes us to live in a state of panic all the time and often causes us to die. At the very least, taking too many risks keeps us from ever having a stable core identity. If I am *always* in a process of huge change and flux, who am I? Worse, who can relate to me?

When I am giving seminars around the country I am invariably asked the question, "How long does it take to get healthy?" I understand the frustration of those who ask. If you had asked me 15 years ago if I would ever be happy with myself, if I would ever be in a clear loving relationship with a woman or if I would ever love the work that I do for a living, my honest answer would have been "No." But I *am* happy with myself, my marriage and my work now. Very happy.

I remember waking up one morning several years ago to the sounds of the geese flying outside our bedroom window. It was one of those tiny, magical moments that come to us now and again. I had a piercing and instant perception and realization. In a split-second that lingered with me warmly for the rest of the day, I realized that I was happy, content and grateful for my marriage, my children, my work and my life. Like all good recovering addicts, I had to pinch myself to make sure it was real, and then I had to listen to the ghosts of my past creep in and try to take it all away by saying, "It won't last. Something awful will happen and take it all away. You don't deserve to be happy. It will get boring. You need to stir something up to create more intensity."

When those ghosts were finished speaking, which I respectfully allowed them to do, I told myself, "John, those are the ghosts of your painful past speaking to you. They're just reminding you from whence you have come. Honor your past, but don't let it run your life now."

The ghosts quieted down, and the rest of my life since then has been just as good.

Have I had crises in my life since then? Of course I have. Have I had problems with the kids, with work and with my own growth and development? Of course I have. Problems are the parts of life that challenge us and keep us fresh and alive. What's different is the way that I interpret the challenges that life offers me. Things that were disasters years ago are now just challenges. Things that would throw me for a loop for days now get handled in a few minutes or hours. It makes life a heck of a lot easier.

And what about risks? What about boredom? I take risks all the time, now, but they aren't the huge, dramatic risks that put my life in danger the way they used to be. I appreciate the wisdom of "trying something different." But "trying something different" doesn't mean tearing up my whole life every year, throwing it away and starting all over. Taking a risk doesn't mean having an affair because Linda borrowed my pen and forgot to return it. A healthy risk might be telling your partner that you wish they'd brush their teeth in the morning before making love, or telling your partner that you appreciate having them in your life and that you value the relationship. It might be intelligently going out on your own to start a business after years of working for other people, or trying to write a book instead of just talking about writing one. A healthy risk could mean ending a painful, stagnant relationship after trying various counseling strategies with no success. Or it could mean giving up the comfort of another one of your addictions.

Life is filled with excitement. There is wonder and awe in the universe. You don't have to ride the space shuttle to find it. Being open to life is what makes it so much fun. Sometimes you can even get more than you bargained for.

Last year we decided to take all of my frequent flyer tickets and go to Jamaica for a Christmas vacation. We had always stayed at home for the entire holiday season, but we had also been intrigued by friends who chose to go away for the holidays. So after a Christmas Eve family gathering with all the relatives, Linda and the kids and I took off Christmas morning at 7:00 a.m. The hotel I had researched so carefully turned out to be a disaster, but after hours and hours of traveling we looked at one another with that look that said, "It's awful, it's too late to do anything about it, we're too tired, let's make the best of it, let's get some sleep."

The next day I went out for my morning jog and halfway through it I told myself that we hadn't traveled this far to be miserable for ten days. In my sweaty jogging clothes I stopped at all of the other hotels in the area until I found a very nice one that had some openings. I brought everyone back to take a look. With big grins on our faces we checked out of the first one and checked into the new one. We had a wonderful vacation the rest of the time.

I had read some articles about Jamaica before we left, and one that particularly fascinated me was about a remote village in the western mountains of Jamaica which was peopled by the descendants of courageous slaves and their leader, Kujo, a brilliant guerrilla tactician, who defeated the British and won their freedom in 1739, well over a hundred years before others on the island were freed. The mountainous area is called Cockpit Country due to the shape of the terrain, and the Jamaican Maroons were the inhabitants of Accompong Village, where I thought I wanted to go. I had also read of a ceremonial drum that local craftsmen made in honor of the drums that were used to communicate while fighting the British. For some reason I felt the need to go to Accompong and see if I could obtain one of those drums. The idea of stepping on ground where a hero such as Kujo had helped win the freedom of slaves that long ago felt powerful to me.

After settling into our hotel and doing some of the typical Minnesota Tourist things, like swimming and local sightseeing, I began to ask local Jamaicans about Accompong and the Maroons, but the answers weren't too reassuring. Most of the people had only vaguely heard of them and those who had heard of Accompong had very different stories to tell.

One woman said that the Maroons were "very short and very tiny," as if she were describing pygmies. A man said that they were a pretty fierce people and I probably wouldn't want to go there. The rumors were fascinating, and with each one, I felt more compelled to find someone to take me there. I was finally able to find a man who was willing to drive me there, and we set off early on the morning of New Year's Eve. I had my map of Jamaica and we stopped and bought a couple of cans of Coke.

Lewis was a real trooper, I must admit. It turned out he thought we were going to a place called Maroon Town, which was on a fairly well-marked road, even on my map. He was pretty surprised when I finally figured out that where I wanted to go and where he was taking me were two different places. We were both very surprised when we got lost after leaving the sugar cane fields at the foot of the mountains. Going literally one mile per hour in his small Japanese van, we found ourselves on a washed out road ascending into breathtaking mountain jungle with absolutely no way to turn around should we meet another vehicle or mule-drawn cart. We passed a man on a mule and Lewis asked in patois if we were heading in the right direction. He stopped once to look at his tires, which I later found out was because one of them was losing air.

He said nervously, "I wonder what we'd do if the van breaks down way up here." I thought, "We'll get back three days from now, if ever." I kept wondering if this was worth it. Maybe Linda and the kids had the right idea when they decided to stay back at the beach.

We finally made it to Accompong Village — three hours to travel 45 miles — but it was worth it indeed. High in the mountains, with crystal clear tropical air and a light breeze blowing, on New Year's Eve, this was a village of people who had struggled for over two centuries to keep their original African way of life intact. Mark, my guide, proudly showed me the village and introduced me to one of the elders. Little children carried my camera and tape recorder and giggled and laughed as we walked. Mark took me out onto the edge of a hill where there stood a regal old silk-cotton tree, the site of the signing of the treaty with the British. He said it was the place that their independence celebration started each year. On the tree was a sign written in an African language: "We Are All Family." A breath of wind blew through the leaves of the giant tree and I felt as if I were 250 years old. It was a reverent and sacred place that moved me every bit as much as if I had been at the Lincoln Memorial in Washington, D.C. Mark pointed far down the hilltop into a quiet ravine to indicate where Kujo was buried. The wind blew again, and then we went back to the village.

Before I left, I bought a marvelous drum from George Huggins, the craftsman whom I had read about. On one side of the drum was inscribed *"Signing Of The Peace Treaty in 1739,"* and on the other, *Mandela Is Free — Maroon Celebrate."*

I'll never forget the looks of surprise on everyone's faces when I walked into our hotel room with my drum in hand. It wasn't a life-threatening trek by any means. But it was something I never would have done a few years ago either. It would have been too inconvenient, too time-consuming, too dangerous or something. I showered and dressed for the Caribbean New Year's Eve celebration we attended that evening.

As my family and I talked, laughed and danced, I realized that all of the good risks that I had taken since the time I began my recovery from being a hurt child had been worth every bit of it, and that my little journey up into the mountains of Jamaica was symbolic not just of a people's freedom from slavery, but of my own freedom from enslavement by alcohol and family dysfunction.

As I sit here at my desk in my office at home, finishing this book, I look over now and then at the drum that George Huggins made by hand to celebrate the independence of the Maroons, and I think back over my life and thank God for every minute of it.

I hope that you find the healthy risks in life, and that you are able to accept their invitation now and then. If you do, you will be richly rewarded in ways that you never dreamed were possible — in the little ways.

BIBLIOGRAPHY

Ackerman, R.J. (1985). **Children Of Alcoholics: Bibliography And Resource Guide.** Indiana, PA: Addiction Research Publishing.

Adams, K. (1991). **Silently Seduced: When Parents Make Their Children Partners.** Deerfield Beach, FL: Health Communications, Inc.

Anderson, L. (1989). **Dear Dad: Letters From An Adult Child.** New York: Viking Penguin.

Bane, V., Grant, M., Alexander, B., Kelly, K., Brown, S.A., Wegher, B., & Feldon-Mitchell, L. (1990). Silent No More. *People*, December 17, 1990.

Bateson, G. (1972). **Steps To An Ecology Of Mind.** O. Chandler Publishing Company.

Becker, E. (1973). **The Denial Of Death.** New York: Macmillan Publishing.

Bem, S.L. (1976). Probing the Promise of Androgyny. In J. Sherman and F. Denmark (Eds.), **Psychology Of Women: Future Directions Of Research.** Psychological Dimensions.

Black, C. (1981). **It Will Never Happen To Me.** Denver: M.A.C. Publishers.

Blake, M. (1988). **Dances With Wolves.** New York: Ballantine Books.

Bly, R. (1990). **Iron John: A Book About Men.** New York: Addison-Wesley Publishing Co.

Bowen, M. (1978). **Family Therapy In Clinical Practice.** New York: Jason Aronsen.

Breskin, D. (1991). Oliver Stone. *Rolling Stone,* April 4, 1991.

Brooks, C. (1981). **The Secret Everyone Knows.** San Diego, CA: The Kroc Foundation.

Brownmiller, S. (1975). **Against Our Will: Men, Women, And Rape.** New York: Simon & Schuster.

Carnes, P. (1987). **Out Of The Shadows.** Minneapolis, MN: Compcare.

Chalberg, C. (1984). Washington's Still on His Pedestal But His Best Advice Isn't Followed. *Minneapolis Star And Tribune,* August 26, 1984.

Cork, M.R. (1969). **The Forgotten Children.** Toronto, Canada: Addiction Research Foundation.

Crichton, M. (1988). **Travels.** New York: Alfred A. Knopf.

Davis, S.O. (1991). Kevin Costner: Myth or Man? *Ladies' Home Journal,* April, 1991.

DeMause, L. (1974). **The History Of Childhood.** New York: Psychohistory Press.

Eisenhart, M.A. & Holland, D.C. (1983). Learning Gender From Peers: The Role of Peer Group in the Cultural Transmission of Gender. *Human Organization,* 42, 321-332.

Ellis, A., & Harper, R.A. (1961). **A Guide To Rational Living.** Englewood, Cliffs, NY: Prentice-Hall.

Erikson, E.H. (1950). **Childhood And Society.** New York: W.W. Norton and Company.

Erikson, E.H. (1968). **Identity: Youth And Crisis.** New York: W.W. Norton and Company.

Erwin, P. (1985). Similarity of Attitudes and Constucts in Children's Friendships. *Journal Of Experimental Child Psychology,* 40, 470-485.

Farrell, W. (1975). **The Liberated Man.** New York: Bantam.

Farrell, W. (1986). **Why Men Are The Way They Are.** New York: McGraw-Hill.

Feng, G.F., & English, J. (1972). Translation of Tao Te Ching by Lao Tsu. New York: Random House.

Fossum, M.A. (1989). **Catching Fire: Men Coming Alive In Recovery.** New York: Harper and Row.

Fossum, M.A., & Mason, M.J. (1986). **Facing Shame: Families In Recovery.** New York, W.W. Norton and Company, Inc.

Friel, C.C. (1948). **The Story of Edward And Margaret Friel.** San Francisco: Charles Camden Friel.

Friel, J.C. (1985). Co-dependency Assessment Inventory: A Preliminary Research Tool. *Focus On Family And Chemical Dependency,* May/June 1985.

Friel, J.C., & Friel, L.D. (1988). **Adult Children: The Secrets Of Dysfunctional Families.** Deerfield Beach, FL: Health Communications, Inc.

Friel, J.C., & Friel, L.D. (1990). **An Adult Child's Guide To What's "Normal."** Deerfield Beach, FL: Health Communications, Inc.

Goldberg, H. (1976). **The Hazards Of Being Male.** New York: Nash Publishing.

Goldberg, H. (1979). **The New Male.** New York: William Morrow.

Gould, R.L. (1978). **Transformations: Growth And Change In Adult Life.** New York: Simon and Schuster, Inc.

Greenfield, M. (1991). The Many Faces of Gorbachev. *Newsweek,* March 4, 1991, 72.

Greenleaf, J. (1981). **Co-Alcoholic, Para-Alcoholic.** Los Angeles: Jael Greenleaf.

Hawking, S. (1988). **A Brief History Of Time: From The Big Bang To Black Holes.** New York: Bantam Books.

Hendrix, H. (1988). **Getting The Love You Want: A Guide For Couples.** New York: Henry Holt and Company.

Huang, C.A. (1991). **Quantum Soup.** Berkeley, CA: Celestial Arts.

Jacklin, C.N. (1989). Female and male: Issues of gender. *American Psychologist*, 44, 127-133.

Jacklin, C.N., & Maccoby, E.E. (1978). Social behavior at 33 months in same-sex and mixed-sex dyads. *Child Development*, 49, 557-569.

Johnson, V.E. (1980). **I'll Quit Tomorrow.** New York: Harper and Row.

Keillor, G. (1985). **Lake Wobegon Days.** New York: Viking Penguin.

Kinsella, W.P. (1983). **Shoeless Joe.** New York: Ballantine Books.

Kipfer, B.A. (1990). **14,000 Things To Be Happy About.** New York: Workman Publishing.

Kohlberg, L. (1966). A Cognitive-Developmental Analysis of Children's Sex-Role Concepts and Attitudes. In E.E. Maccoby (Ed.), **The Development Of Sex Differences.** Stanford, CA: Stanford University Press.

Kraft, L.W., & Vraa, C.W. (1975). Sex Composition Of Groups and Patterns of Self-Disclosure by High School Females. *Psychological Reports*, 37, 733-734.

Kundtz, David J. (1991). **Men And Feelings. Understanding The Male Experience.** Deerfield Beach, FL: Health Communications, Inc.

Lao Tsu. **Tao Te Ching.** Feng, G.F. and English, J., translators. New York: Random House.

Leerhsen, C. & Wright, L. (1991). L.A.'s Violent New Video. *Newsweek*, March 18, 1991, 53.

Levinson, D.J. (1978). **The Seasons Of A Man's Life.** New York: Alfred A. Knopf, Inc.

Maccoby, E.E. (1990). Gender and Relationships: A Developmental Account. *American Psychologist*, 45, 513-520.

Maccoby, E.E., & Jacklin, C.N. (1974). **The Psychology Of Sex Differences.** Stanford, CA: Stanford University Press.

Maccoby, E.E., & Jacklin, C.N. (1987). Gender Segregation in Childhood. In H.W. Reese (Ed.), **Advances In Child Development And Behavior** (Vol. 20, pp. 239-288). New York: Academic Press.

Maltz, D.N., & Borker, R.A. (1983). A Cultural Approach to Male-Female Miscommunication. In John A. Gumperz (Ed.), **Language and Social Identity.** New York: Cambridge University Press.

Maslow, A.H. (1954). **Motivation And Personality.** New York: Harper and Brothers.

McDonnell, L. (1991). Sexual politics. *Minneapolis/St. Paul Magazine*, February, 1991, 32.

Miller, A. (1983). **For Your Own Good: Hidden Cruelty In Childrearing And The Roots Of Violence.** New York: Farrar Strauss Giroux.

Miller, A. (1984). **Thou Shalt Not Be Aware: Society's Betrayal Of The Child.** New York: Farrar Strauss Giroux.

Minuchin, S. (1974). **Families And Family Therapy.** Cambridge: Harvard University Press.

Peck, R.C. (1968). Psychological Developments in the Second Half of Life. In B.L. Neugarten (Ed.) **Middle Age And Aging.** Chicago: University of Chicago Press.

Piaget, J. (1936). **The Origin Of Intelligence In Children.** New York: International Universities Press.

Piaget, J. (1950). **The Pyschology Of Intelligence.** New York: Harcourt & Brace.

Rader, D. (1991). I Want To Be Like My Dad. *Parade*. January 20, 1991.

Rosen, M., & Johnson, T. (1990). Pack Leader. *People*, November 19, 1990, 138-143.

Ryan, M. (1990). A Simple Deed With Awesome Power. *Parade*, August 19, 1990.

Salholz, E., Clift, E., Springen, K., & Johnson, P. (1990). Women Under Assault. *Newsweek*, July 16, 1990, 23-24.

212 • The Grown-Up Man

Satir, V. (1967). **Conjoint Family Therapy.** Palo Alto, CA: Science and Behavior Books.

Scarf, M. (1987). **Intimate Partners: Patterns In Love And Marriage.** New York: Random House.

Sheehy, G. (1974). **Passages: Predictable Crises Of Adult Life.** New York: E.P. Dutton.

Smalley, S. (1982). **Co-dependency: An Introduction.** New Brighton, MN: Sondra Smalley.

Steinbeck, J. (1939). **The Grapes Of Wrath.** New York: Viking Press.

Subby, R.C. (1987). **Lost In The Shuffle: The Co-Dependent Reality.** Deerfield Beach, FL: Health Communications, Inc.

Thorne, B. (1986). Girls and Boys Together, But Mostly Apart. In W.W. Hartup & L. Rubin (Eds.), **Relationships And Development.** Hillsdale, NJ: Erlbaum.

Wegscheider-Cruse, S. (1981). **Another Chance: Hope And Health For The Alcoholic Family.** Palo Alto, CA: Science and Behavior Books.

Wholey, D. (1984). **The Courage To Change.** Boston: Houghton Mifflin.

Will, G. (1991). Slamming The Doors. *Newsweek*, March 25, 1991.

Winkler, A.C. (1987). **The Lunatic.** Kingston, Jamaica: Kingston Publishers Limited.

Woititz, J.G. (1983). **Adult Children Of Alcoholics.** Deerfield Beach, FL: Health Communications, Inc.

Zilbergeld, B. (1978). **Male Sexuality.** New York: Little, Brown and Company.

CLINIC
NATIONAL LOCATIONS/
CONTACT AGENICES

The Lifeworks Clinic is a special 4-day program designed to help us discover and work through the family-of-origin roots of our *self-defeating patterns of living.*

The Lifeworks Clinic is offered in several major metropolitan areas throughout the country. Prices, insurance reimbursement, schedules and lodging arrangements may vary.

St. Paul/Minneapolis, MN
Friel & Associates/Lifeworks
612/482-7982

Sioux City, IA
Gordon Center
712/279-3960

Orange County, CA
Pathways to Discovery
714/964-2267

Dayton/Cincinnati, OH
New Life Family Workshops
513/258-2607

Oklahoma City, OK
Norman Recovery Center
405/359-5368

Miami, FL
Family Passages
305/665-0212

Houston, TX
Recovery Source
713/338-4000

The majority of lectures at each location are presented by **John Friel,** except Houston, where John is available for half of the clinics.

AUDIOTAPES AVAILABLE FROM FRIEL & ASSOCIATES/LIFEWORKS

**Co-Dependency: The Search for Wholeness
(4 audiocassettes)** $28.00

**Adult Children from Dysfunctional Families
(3 audiocassettes)** $21.00

**Separateness and Intimacy/Sexuality and Spirituality
(2 audiocassettes)** $14.00

Make checks payable to Friel & Associates. Send order to 4176 North Lexington Avenue, St. Paul, MN 55126
Call or write for updates on tapes or clinics.

MEN'S ISSUES IN THE '90s

THE FLYING BOY:
Healing The Wounded Man
John Lee

This record of one man's journey to find his "true masculinity" and his way out of co-dependent and addictive relationships is of help to all men.
ISBN 1-55874-006-6 .... $7.95

RECOVERY: PLAIN AND SIMPLE
John Lee

A collection of John Lee's talks over the past two years deal with addictive relationships, adult child issues, dysfunctional families and co-dependency.
ISBN 1-55874-108-9 .... $7.95

MEN AND FEELINGS:
Understanding The Male Experience
David J. Kundtz

Men And Feelings: Understanding The Male Experience is designed to help men understand more clearly what feelings are, the way feelings work, or don't work, and why.
ISBN 1-55874-143-7 .... $5.95

THE GROWN-UP MAN: Hope •
Hurt • Honor • Heroes • Healing
John Friel, Ph.D.

Friel summarizes classical psychological literature in men's and women's studies and discusses how men have been hurt by too much mothering and not enough fathering.
ISBN 1-55874-179-8 .... $9.95

SOOTHING MOMENTS: Daily
Meditations For Fast-Track Living
Bryan Robinson, Ph.D.

Soothing Moments is for those leading fast-paced and highly-pressured lifestyles who need time out each day to restore joy, peace and serenity in their lives.
ISBN 1-55874-075-9 .... $6.95

MEN SPEAK OUT: In The Heart
Of Men's Recovery: Six Dialogues
For, By And About Conscious Men
David Lenfest, Ph.D.

These dialogues conducted with six men who are leaders in the men's movement and in recovery give a concise overview of The Men's Movement.
ISBN 1-55874-166-6 .... $8.95

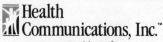

Health
Communications, Inc.™
1-800-441-5569

New Books . . .
from Health Communications

HEAL YOUR SELF-ESTEEM: Recovery From Addictive Thinking
Bryan Robinson, Ph.D.

Do you have low self-esteem? Do you blame others for your own unhappiness? If so, you may be an addictive thinker. The 10 Principles For Healing, an innovative, positive approach to recovery, are integrated into this book to provide a new attitude with simple techniques for recovery.

ISBN 1-55874-119-4 $9.95

HEALING ENERGY: The Power Of Recovery
Ruth Fishel, M.Ed., C.A.C.

Linking the newest medical discoveries in mind/body/spirit connections with the field of recovery, this book illustrates how to balance ourselves mentally, physically and spiritually to overcome our addictive behavior.

ISBN 1-55874-128-3 $9.95

CREDIT, CASH AND CO-DEPENDENCY: The Money Connection
Yvonne Kaye, Ph.D.

Co-dependents and Adult Children seem to experience more problems than most as money can be used as an anesthetic or fantasy. Yvonne Kaye writes of the particular problems the co-dependent has with money, sharing her own experiences.

ISBN 1-55874-133-X $9.95

THE LAUNDRY LIST: The ACoA Experience
Tony A. and Dan F.

Potentially The Big Book of ACoA, *The Laundry List* includes stories, history and helpful information for the Adult Child of an alcoholic. Tony A. discusses what it means to be an ACoA and what the self-help group can do for its members.

ISBN 1-55874-105-4 $9.95

LEARNING TO SAY NO: Establishing Healthy Boundaries
Carla Wills-Brandon, M.A.

If you grew up in a dysfunctional family, establishing boundaries is a difficult and risky decision. Where do you draw the line? Learn to recognize yourself as an individual who has the power to say no.

ISBN 1-55874-087-2 $8.95

3201 S.W. 15th Street,
Deerfield Beach, FL 33442-8190
1-800-851-9100

Health
Communications, Inc.®

Other Books By . . .
Health Communications

ADULT CHILDREN OF ALCOHOLICS (Expanded)
Janet Woititz

Over a year on *The New York Times* Best-Seller list, this book is the primer on Adult Children of Alcoholics.

ISBN 1-55874-112-7   **$8.95**

STRUGGLE FOR INTIMACY
Janet Woititz

Another best-seller, this book gives insightful advice on learning to love more fully.

ISBN 0-932194-25-7   **$6.95**

BRADSHAW ON: THE FAMILY: A Revolutionary Way of Self-Discovery
John Bradshaw

The host of the nationally televised series of the same name shows us how families can be healed and individuals can realize full potential.

ISBN 0-932194-54-0   **$9.95**

HEALING THE SHAME THAT BINDS YOU
John Bradshaw

This important book shows how toxic shame is the core problem in our compulsions and offers new techniques of recovery vital to all of us.

ISBN 0-932194-86-9   **$9.95**

HEALING THE CHILD WITHIN: Discovery and Recovery for
Adult Children of Dysfunctional Families — Charles Whitfield, M.D.

Dr. Whitfield defines, describes and discovers how we can reach our Child Within to heal and nurture our woundedness.

ISBN 0-932194-40-0   **$8.95**

A GIFT TO MYSELF: A Personal Guide To Healing My Child Within
Charles L. Whitfield, M.D.

Dr. Whitfield provides practical guidelines and methods to work through the pain and confusion of being an Adult Child of a dysfunctional family.

ISBN 1-55874-042-2   **$11.95**

HEALING TOGETHER: A Guide To Intimacy And Recovery For
Co-dependent Couples — Wayne Kritsberg, M.A.

This is a practical book that tells the reader why he or she gets into dysfunctional and painful relationships, and then gives a concrete course of action on how to move the relationship toward health.

ISBN 1-55784-053-8   **$8.95**

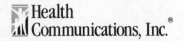

3201 S.W. 15th Street,
Deerfield Beach, FL 33442-8190
1-800-851-9100

Health Communications, Inc.®